Book of the Highest Good: Volume 6

The Amarna Experience

By Joyce McCartney

The Book of the Highest Good, Volume 6

The Amarna Experience

Copyright: May, 2014 by Joyce McCartney

Cover Design by Adam Brown

Drawings are sketches by the author and Adam Brown

Produced by Positive Options, Inc.

Print Version: ISBN-13 978-0-9897088-9-0

E-book Version: ISBN-13 978-0-9904776-0-0

Printed on demand by Amazon.com First Edition, 2014

Kindle Version by Amazon.com First Edition, 2014

Table of Contents

The Book of the Highest Good: The Series.................1

Preface..5

Chapter One: The Rise and Fall of Maat.....................8

Chapter Two: The Miracle of Amarna......................13

Chapter Three: Maat Thrives 23

Chapter Four: As Amarna Was, So Goes the Future ..44

Chapter Five: Seeds of Amarna Sown Once Again 51

Chapter Six: If Walls Could Speak 59

Chapter Seven: Play It Again, Soul 76

Chapter Eight: Will Love, No Harm 88

Chapter Nine: Do It Again in Dogon.........................99

Acknowledgements 111

The Book of the Highest Good: The Series

Book 1: A Beginning Experience

In this book, the author faces the universal experience of making sense of grief-filled setbacks in her life and finds that she has two minds at work on the problem. One is the Conscious Mind of fear and regret and the other is the Higher Mind of peace and love. Choosing to focus on the Higher Mind, calling it the Peaceful One, and to ignore the Conscious Mind called, The Fearful One, she begins to ask questions about how life unfolds. She discovers that she is conversing with her Soul, which has the plan for her life and the resources to guide her in living a life of peace and happiness.

Book 2: Walk to Freedom

In this book, the author continues her conversation with the Peaceful One and discovers the power of forgiveness, trust in the intention for the Highest Good, how to understand seeming accidents, and the inner world of animals. Once forgiveness is embraced, one has the opportunity to live in freedom and to be happy. There is also a tantalizing look at how contact with one's Higher Mind can be used to solve practical problems of living one's life in peace. The Travelers is a dialogue between two people each asking questions for the other to channel the answer from their Higher Minds, or Soul.

Book 3: Being of Light

Once one can consistently contact the Higher Mind, one has access to vast amounts of benign and reliable information otherwise unknowable to the Conscious Mind. In this book the author asks The Peaceful One about the health of the human body, the nature of the human aura, the workings of atoms, electricity, and the original creation of the physical existence. Towards the end of the book, an ancient pharaoh speaks who begins to explain how the golden age of Egypt was founded upon the intention for the Highest Good.

Book 4: Channeled Tour of Ancient Egypt

The founding of a small town of mud huts that was later to become the mighty Egyptian nation is described. It is essentially the story of a family, beginning with the role of a mother who sets the founding intention of the Highest Good even before the birth of her son who later leads his people to peace. With such a good foundation, the unfolding of events bring to light how the small boy could learn to levitate stones, cure the sick and injured, and advise rulers how to create an environment of prosperity for their nations. We hear stories of everyday life and descriptions of the journey of the soul painted on underground walls. Finally, we have the nature of the

2

Highest Good portrayed across the globe in a plan for peace in the modern age. This plan, left for us to find by the ancient Egyptians, is now reborn as a model for modern citizens of peace.

Book 5: Stars Over Egypt

The question of extraterrestrial contact in ancient times is resolved in this book, telling of a Higher Mind contact with beings, the Hathors, who congregate in spirit form around certain stars and planets. It is from these benign etheric beings that much technology and science was learned. In order to understand contact with these beings, the nature of a friendly relationship is discussed, as well as the need to continually release fear, doubt, and regret. A clear channel only exists through a free and joyful outlook on life. Once contact with other dimensions is made, much good information can be put to use for the Plan for Peace.

Lastly a charming story of an ancient lifetime of Edgar Cayce as RaTa is told, illustrating how peace can be made in every transaction of life, even to the point of rejuvenation of the body.

Book 6: The Amarna Experience

The Egyptian town of Amarna was founded in the middle dynastic period on a previously unused site. It was located between the highly developed communities in the north and south, which had lost the belief in Maat. In this book, we are told the story of Akhenaten and his family who were not welcome in the north or the south because their ideas of the Highest Good were not in favor at the time. Thus Akhenaten left his family behind and found a barren place between the north and the south towns. He lived alone in the desert to begin all over again to trust the Highest Good. Read along with us and see how he learned to contact the star beings for help to find water, raise a crop, reconnect with his family, and found a thriving community based on peaceful living. This community eventually seeded other civilizations all over the world with peace. As a model of how anyone can do the same today, this story lights a beacon of peace beyond no other to anyone who yearns to find peace, live in peace and give peace to others.

Preface

When one enters into the unknown world of the Higher Mind, one must suppose that wondrous things would happen. But imagine my delight when I am given the simple story of a family of religious refugees determined to build a good life for themselves, and to give the truth of peace back to the world from which they were evicted. Imagine my surprise to find that I was one of them and that I continue to do today what I did in ancient times on my own farm in the rural Midwest.

After years of learning how to access this Higher Mind information, I have found that all of my efforts to channel information from my soul are devoted to making peace. Peace of the mind, the heart, and the community is such a grand thing that the star beings have conspired to bring this information forward at this time. They come to give once again the great gift that peace is. For peace gives as much to the participants as to all others who come to inquire. Giving no harm and much good, it is indeed a sign of the Highest Good at work. The message of this book is to find contentment with just being at peace, for peace is an access to a cosmic agreement that has an energy of its own. It has the power to heal and rejuvenate and it will easily come when there are no barriers to its propagation.

And so, it is with joy for the simple things of life done very well in peace, that I proceed on this small laptop to tell not a grand story of love and war, but a story of a small family created in peace which grows into a nation revived over and over again in peace so as to last for many more thousands of years of peace and prosperity.

We begin with The Revered Healer who was introduced in *Book of the Highest Good, Vol. 4, A Channeled Tour of Ancient Egypt*. He was the son of the Great Mother who began the story in the first place. Even before her child was born, this mother set her intention for only the Highest Good to come to her life and those of her children. Finding that she was pregnant once again, she prayed that only the Highest Good should result from this new life and thus it unfolded as she requested. The image of her sitting by a fire with the intention for the Highest Good on her mind became the symbol for *Maat*, meaning *the order of the universe*. Now her son returns in this story, many thousands of years later, to tell the rest of the story of what he started.

This part of the story of Egypt was begun during the period of the recorded Pharaohs, which is much better documented than the beginning history of Egypt. During this period, the Egyptians and indeed much of the ancient world enjoyed a standardized language, and had scribes who named and recorded the succession of pharaohs and the events of their days. At the time of the recorded Pharaohs, the intention for the Highest Good was being lost and Egyptians were fostering an unequal society based self-gain and conflict. But since the original intention for the Highest Good carries so much power, there is, in the middle of Egypt's history, a reversal event that guides them to return to the origins of the peace that was planned at the founding of their society. Let's listen to the story of how an apparent failure is turned into both a revival and an improvement of the plan for peace.

Chapter One:
The Rise and Fall of Maat

Joyce: I want to know more about how the early beginnings of a peaceful Egypt turned out. There was so much time and so many people were involved over thousands of years. How did they manage to keep the principles of Maat intact that would keep them in peace?

The Revered Healer: Within the time frame between the end of the mostly undocumented ancient times of Egypt and the highly recorded times of the rule of the Pharaohs called the Dynastic Periods, there were many centuries of peace in Egyptian society. For most Egyptians living during these peaceful times, there was little concern that anything would be amiss, as their work and families were protected by the rule of the principle of the Highest Good. The pharaohs were humble, but capable people from their own ranks who organized and adjudicated only as the Highest Good would direct. And indeed this period was very prosperous and lasted many thousands of years longer than is currently thought.

However, later things changed. Although the common people were still largely unaffected by the nature of the concerns of the priests and their followers, the developing royal families, of which we will tell much more at a later time, were beginning to think that allowing harm was justifiable if their needs could be advanced. Within the temple grounds during these later recorded dynastic periods, there were many who did not follow the ancient teachings of how Maat was to be administered in each and every transaction of daily life. These ancient teachings had always leveled society to a desirable unity of thought and purpose, which resulted in significant prosperity, monument building, and the transfer of science and technology from celestial beings. With the few who did not want this level society to continue, however, harm began to reappear for everyone. The idea spread that some people were made superior to others and therefore entitled to more wealth and power. Their numbers grew and the administrative classes, who were educated in the increasingly standardized hieroglyphic language, were the first to step forward and declare themselves to be a middle and even a ruling class.

First and foremost, changing from a classless society to a two- or even three-class society required that a member of the the upper class be addressed with a double name such as Mut, the Administrator, as well as Mut, Master of Painters. As these double names proliferated and created positions of status, there were some who objected and fled. Others, who wished to participate in the changing system, stayed. Those who fled anticipated the dire consequences of the decline of the practice of Maat. Once known to be a depiction of a mother preparing a meal for her family with the intention for the Highest Good in mind, the symbol of Maat later came to mean order, such as the original Creator gave order that was good for all. With the rising conflict between classes, however, much of the original intention and teaching was lost. Those who stayed obeyed all of the strict rules and regulations, making tribute payments to temple coffers that formerly were closely regulated for the common good by the principle of Maat and dispersed to those in need. As the old practices changed, the administrators kept the money and built large houses and businesses that they hoped would prosper. In time, the consequences of these newer practices began to appear and there was a reversal of prosperity, for the leaders did not enjoy the support of all of the people because did they did not serve the needs of all of the people. The great prosperity began to fail as the Revered Healer had always said that it would.

In those days, there were none who had read and understood the ancient texts more completely than the foreigners who paid tribute in gold and diamonds for access to certain kinds of technical information made known through the Hathor speakers. Such information was about useful things such as how to find good water and easily dig wells to irrigate the land. Such things were useful for the general populace and when the foreigners asked their questions and took the information back home (mainly to other parts of Africa) they prospered, in contrast to what was beginning to happen in Egypt.

Thus a moment of truth in the form of a reversal event was forecast in the messages from the star beings so that all could reevaluate and reform their intentions. Having no interest in maintaining Maat, the Egyptians lost contact with the Hathors. This critical event just happened to be on the last moon of the anniversary season of the founding of ancient Egypt about; 13,000 B.C. It was a moment of great sadness and disappointment for those who had founded the practice of Maat to see from the etheric realm. They saw that all that they had provided in peace was in reversal, and on their anniversary. As a result, the Hathors sent one of their own to incarnate into physical form to remind those in power in Egypt about their responsibilities for observing the Highest Good in all dealings and to alert all to the coming demise of all that they held sacred and dear.

It was by means of just such a man that the cult of Akhenaten was founded and the old ways were revived in small groups and openly practiced. The differences between the old and new practices were vivid. Soon none of those versed in the corrupt ways wanted Akhenaten and his family in either the north or the south cities practicing the new beliefs. Akhenaten and his small group planned to leave in peace and find a new home in between the northern and the southern cities. Unknown to them, this small beginning would be the future city of Amarna. As far as they knew at the time, it was a place that had no name and few resources, except sand, stars, and sun.

With such a bold move as to re-found the ancient pure Egyptian culture all over again, Akhenaten had given the corrupt Egyptians a view of what repair was needed Not wishing to harm the existing society, however, the pious and gentle man known as Akhenaten left for the desert to be constituted pharaoh of Maat for only his own clan. With that, he planned to renounce all but the ceremonial functions associated with his title, asking to be included in all of the work and duties as the previous, humble pharaohs were. He knew that his household was destined to prosper for it was founded on the ancient principle of Maat, the order of the universe.

Joyce: This is interesting. Akhenaten intended to return to the pure, original teachings of his homeland and to do that, he reverted to a classless society model and set out on his own to rebuild it. I can see how he had great trust in the Highest Good. I have learned the same thing. There were times when I had no other option but to trust the Highest Good and things always worked out much better than I expected. But he is just one man with a small family. I am curious to see how he could revive a great society with such a small start. I want to learn more!

Chapter Two:
The Miracle of Amarna

Revered Healer: The miracle of Amarna is not so much that it existed, but how it was developed by so few and had such a large effect. It saved a great nation from defeat and spread the seeds of peace all over the world. Such can be done again, today, in any nation, for the methods of communication are now much better. So let us look at the methods of making peace as they were in those days and acquire the knowledge of how they can be used the same today to promote peace.

When Amarna was founded, there was nothing at the site to recommend it as a great place, for it was a wide band of sand far enough from the river Nile, that if the power of peace were ever to be tested, this would be the place. It was a place where no one ever came but, once peace had its way, no one ever wanted to leave.

For peace to prosper it needed a great conversation to occur between Akhenaten and the Hathors in which a great plan was laid and much information was given as to the ways and means to accomplish such grace in such a forlorn place. At first, Akhenaten, who came to Amarna completely alone, was not aware of his purpose which had been arranged in a pre-life conference; rather he thought that he was fleeing a situation that he could not tolerate. Thus he arrived with little more than a jug or two of water and a small bag of supplies. His own family stayed behind and waited for word from him. And so, he sat lonely and underfed, but proceeded to open his mind to the fact that this was his choice and that it would be a good one for him and his family.

Thus he established himself in peace with his situation. At that point, he had little else to do, but to point to the star system of his intention, Sirius, and declare his mind open to their wide embrace. The star beings residing in its solar system did not come immediately, but as the hours passed through the long night, he sat contentedly and stayed open to them. Finally, his Higher Mind invited him to fall asleep. While he slept, his body was made more compatible to the transmission of knowledge in order to prepare him for the contact that was to come. Many nights were spent this way, and many days were spent collecting water from the mists and eating the little bugs and lizards that offered themselves to support him.

He knew these to be good signs that the Highest Good or Maat, as they called it then, was responding. The response was not what he expected, but rather gave him little steps and increments of grief relief, support, and sustenance. In time, his faith in the little things gave him trust in the bigger gift that was to come. Late one night, as he stared at the star, Sirius, his mind opened and he saw one point of light that emerged from all others as the presence of his chosen friends, the Hathors.

From that one event, the rest of the story unfolds much the same way as it had for his forefathers. In their first transmission, the Hathors laid out a much-needed way to find good, reliable water. They recommended digging a series of ditches and layering them with small rocks and gravel so that the water level under the ground would be encouraged to rise. Akhenaten followed the instructions and, indeed, the water began to dampen the soil. In observing several trenches, he identified where his best source of water was and dug a shallow well.

The shallow well began to bubble with spring water and he wished to improve it with a deeper well. But, as digging a deep well was a very dangerous thing to do alone, he was supported even more by a wandering band of desert travelers arriving with the same need for water. Finding that he had a small source for water that could be improved by digging deeper, they lent their efforts to help. Soon they had all of the water that they wanted and the wanderers planned to wander off once again. They did not leave, however, without asking the critical question: Why was he there and how did he know to dig the small trenches and to line them with stones?

To satisfy their curiosity, he had to stay them from their journey a while longer to explain all that he knew about the long story of Egypt and the use of the Highest Good to reach the Hathors. They were amazed and saw the potential for a lot of good, and so they decided to return once again at a later time to further support him. But then they left and he was alone once again.

This time, while he was alone with plenty of water to drink, he was nonetheless always hungry so he opened once again to the Hathors. He asked the Hathors who came to him regularly every evening at this point, how to provide this place with food not only for himself, but his family and the visitors who had promised to return. At once the Hathors gave a sure way to propagate the few seeds that he had left in his small bag of supplies. These included a few seeds of grain with which he was familiar and some seeds of herbs and grasses that animals would want to eat. Thus he was instructed to soak all of them in some water until they swelled. Next, he needed some dirt with minerals so as to stimulate the seeds to put out roots.

He was instructed to place some mineral-bearing remains of his insect meals in the cup of water with the seeds. With this done, he waited a few days and the seeds began to extend their roots. The roots were strong with the desire to find and hold onto ground. Akhenaten laid them down flat on ground made muddy by watering. He then placed some strips of fabric over them to shade them from the sun. Each day, he put more and more wet dirt over the sprouting seeds and roots until they were mounded up and strong enough to hold the plant upright.

He was instructed to hold the plant in the shape of a droplet wrapped in some scraps of fabric and to dip them in the water each day until the shoots were wrapped around the dirt and fabric and the plant top heavy. Then he split them into two and two again and again until he had many small plants, all of them wrapped in wet dirt and fabric.

Finally, he planted them in the shade of a rock to grow for a week, watering them each hour of the day until they bloomed and started forming their own seeds. As soon as the seeds were viable, he replanted them, doing so over and over until all of the available shaded space had beautiful plants growing much good food. He then had the problem of how to make more shade for the plants, as the sun was very intense in that place, so he asked the Hathors what to do. They said to take the stems of the discarded plants and weave them into little umbrellas for each plant until he had enough fibers for a whole piece of cloth to stretch from rock to rock. Soon he had shaded gardens producing food and more seeds for planting.

Even the small bugs and lizards multiplied from the leftover seeds, giving him even more fertilizer and meat. Eventually, he had a fine piece of cloth, which worked very well as shade. One day, the sun set behind a bank of clouds and some rain fell, disturbing the shady cloth. After he picked it up, he found that the dirt that clung to the cloth provided even more shade, so he left the dirt on the cloth, adding more dust and sand.

Thus the original small supply of seeds had prospered so well that when Akhenaten's wandering band of friends returned, he had much water and grain to feed them and even traded for some much needed tools and additional seeds. Soon it was obvious that the prosperity of one enhanced the prosperity of the other and they became great friends. And because of his sense of responsibility to feed them whenever they stopped by, the travelers made a point to tell many others that they met to also stop by and to give his Hathor readings a try. Thus he traded his readings of solutions of many problems for other much needed items and help.

Soon there was an oasis of green flowing grasses and herbs, but no trees. Although there were some acacia trees nearby, Akhenaten wanted trees that produced nuts and fruits, so he sent word with his traveling friends and to his family to come with sapling trees from their hometown. When they arrived, they found him in good health with a small hut made from mud and sand and good food to eat. They all celebrated and planted the trees which grew rapidly into towering shade trees giving much additional food which was shared with all who came to visit. They all saw the value of always welcoming strangers and feeding them. People found that it worked so well, especially in the desert where resources were scarce, that it was to be the local, longstanding custom required of all men and women.

Once, while entering into the sleep state, he thought that he heard his mother calling him to roast some grain for the evening meal. Akhenaten knew that they who had founded Egypt (the Revered Healer and his family) were calling him to do a service. He left his pillow and went outside under the stars to listen to the words that were coming to him. They said for him to return to the old teachings of Maat and to call this place

Amarna, meaning "scratching out a small start." With this instruction, he realized that he himself had been using Maat and very well at that. He prayed for his countrymen and the whole nation to enjoy the same blessing. Then he went back to bed very satisfied indeed.

With that prayer intact, his attention to the instructions from the Hathors and the intentions for Maat repeated over and over each day, Akhenaten soon was told that he would be given another child. When that child arrived, it grew well on its mother's milk for she was well fed and well treated by her husband. In fact, the leftover milk was given to the other children and even her husband, as breast milk was known to be very nutritious, especially from a well cared-for mother. And so their family grew.

Soon the whole enterprise was so prosperous and happy that visitors came everyday and much trading was carried on. As the children grew, they collected many things from faraway places that had been traded or gifted and used them for play and learning. Soon enough information and artifacts were collected to see the need to start a school. His daughters had married strong and sturdy men who wanted to live at the peaceful place, so soon there were many children, homes and marriages, and then more children. The wives discussed the project and decided to pool their resources and time to do the best job of educating their children. In this manner, the wives developed a small school, which everyone welcomed.

Thus one woman was selected to be the teacher and her other duties were shared by other women so that she would be free to teach and to learn herself. Every visitor was a welcome source of something new and the teacher mother listened intently to the conversations with travelers around the campfires, asking many questions. Although she had learned much of the world from the travelers, she wanted to learn from the Hathors as well, so Akhenaten taught her how to talk with them and she began to ask all kinds of questions about how the universe worked. She taught all she learned to the children, who also learned to talk with the Hathors. With that being common, there was among them not a single one who could not do algebra, geometry, math, and astronomy. Thus the urge to build structures arose to put these skills to work.

They asked the Hathors to suggest a monument to Maat that would make them proud and give more Maat to all who came. The Hathors suggested a long hall of many pillars and rooms for all to come and display their wares on market day as well as to serve the functions of the priests who would later adjudicate disputes, recommend healing and remedies, educate people, trade wisdom with travelers, and organize the ceremonies that preserved the traditions. The function of these skilled priests or administrators would be to provide the growing population with organizational structure and social services. All of this would be housed in the Great Hall building.

Thus the construction of the long hall was started, following the directions of the Hathors, and all went well including the hauling of large stones from a nearby quarry. This time the Hathors had a suggestion different than levitation. They suggested that the larger stones carry the small stones and vice versa. Therefore a gravel road was made and the large stones rolled on the gravel like marbles and when the marbles were about to wear out, they transported more on the back of the large stones, refilled the roads and continued on. Thus more was made out of less and less was made to be more and so forth.

Following the construction of the Great Hall, there was a celebration with flags and many poles bearing the insignia of the town – a small seed, and a lizard – for from such small resources so much was made. That was essentially their definition of Maat: how seeds and lizards led them to be a great town.

We trust that the story is never ended. Then, as now, there is always a need, a small resource, and an opening to Higher Mind with which to raise a new nation of peace. This is the essence of the story of Amarna, except to say that there are those among the recent returnees who have had similar experiences and know very well how, and why, it works. Indeed, it will be a relatively easy task to educate the masses on the principle of Matt. For those who have lacked education want it badly and those who have been discarded by society want badly to be included. Those who have been bombed want peace and those abused for their gender, want equality. Thus whatever is needed is due for much abundance once the right intention for the Highest Good is made and kept in mind for a long enough period of time without doubt.

Doubt has been at work in all actions of greed, evil, and harm since the beginning of man's life on this earth and it is about to end in this century. For peace is not an option to behold and then to doubt. Rather it is a reality that has a life of its own and occurs almost anywhere if only left alone and freed from doubt. We would concur that once one has a need and one requests abundance, only the water of the same good intention and adequate shade from doubt is required for success. Thus we end this chapter as the relief of yet another beautiful sunset is upon us.

Joyce: Seeds and lizards. Although you won't find me eating lizards any time soon, I have to say that this is a heart-warming story. What a tale of good things grown from virtually nothing! Anyone who has suffered great losses should take heart to know that this man voluntarily left all behind to experience everything from nothing. It gives me comfort and security to know that no matter where I am or what conditions there are, that help is always available in such wise form. Since the universe is wired for good, it must always have good available to give.

Chapter Three:
Maat Thrives

Revered Healer: While still in its infancy, there was another resident of the growing town of Amarna, the wife of Akhenaten, a woman named Gentle Ruler or Nefertiti. It was her experience of managing farming and rural businesses that helped the town to further prosper. The people found her to be wise, and indeed gentle. As she loved babies and children, she eventually consorted with Akhenaten to produce a large family of very beautiful children, one of which was named, Man of the Healing Arts. Gentle Ruler loved him and had him trained in all manner of the care and treatment of the body. There was another child, a small boy, Tutankhamen, who was retarded and needed much guidance even to manage everyday tasks. Following the old principles, she gave her son, with little capacity, the best of care. Her other son, the healer, applied many treatments and greatly advanced his brother's abilities. Together they assured him a good life doing the service that he could. Indeed, there were many who allowed that he was of no use, but she followed the old principles of Maat and lavished the best of care on the least capable of all of the people. In time, Tutankhamen grew to be a man of gentle manners and reasonably good intelligence, but hardly able to rule. The people started calling her Great Mother, which was discovered to be her soul name.

The people noticed her application of Maat and declared that, if the least among this large family was treated so favorably, then there must be nothing to fear for having a large family themselves. Thus many parents elected to have many children who ultimately prospered. Thus the town grew into a thriving society based upon peace. In the meantime, great things were developing in other parts of the world and the many who came to visit Egypt saw the vivid contrast between the two societies in Egypt, one following the ancient principles of Maat and the other not.

Joyce: I just love what Nefertiti did. She was a true mother, wise and gentle. But what was special about Akhenaten and why did he do such a thing as to go to a desert and start a civilization all over again?

Revered Healer: It was with one mind that we on the etheric side supported his entrance into this lifetime. We let the lifetime begin for him as a small child, one of twelve children who loved being in a large family. He was a remarkable observer of nature and grew to be a tall, slim, and lovely man with very elongated facial features, much like those on the standing figures on Easter Island. Such a body form reflected the image of the Arturians.

As Akhenaten approached the age of maturity, he wanted his mother to arrange for him to see a girl for his future wife, but she resisted saying that his duty needed to be done for Maat first. As this was much against his will, he soon headed for a retreat in order to find his way in peace. With a great head for the stars, he made his first contact with the Star Beings who informed him of the necessity of his being the teacher of the gifts of the sun. Knowing this, he was reinvigorated and with the assurance that indeed he would be the father of a large and loving family, he continued to develop his understanding of the rule of Maat so that he could add much to the practice of it in Amarna.

Joyce: Akhenaten is famous for his image of a sun disk with little arms out stretched as if giving something. What was the importance of the teaching of the gifts of the sun? Were these teachings known before?

Revered Healer: You have given not one but two questions which cannot be answered at once. Therefore, let us tell yet another story about the sun's rays. They were always honored as a gift of God, but their meaning was not well understood. When he was a small boy, Akhenaten was observing the setting sun and wondered about how much he missed it during the night. When day began, he had much to do, but he yearned to observe it in peace for a longer period of time. Therefore, he took one day to himself and did nothing but observe what the sun did for the Earth. And in doing so, he found that nothing that the sun touched was left unchanged. It touched every point of Earth except underground and the darkness of night. He even noticed that the moon was graced by the sun's rays and used them to reflect back to the Earth new kinds of softer light at night.

With this readily in his mind, Akhenaten wondered about how these rays are made and the Hathors showed him a mental image of an array of little round orbs spraying out from the sun into space traveling in straight lines. He saw them as rays of light and depicted them having little hands extending from the rays of the sun, giving gifts. Thus he created the image of his famous picture of the sun disk and rays on the back of his chairs and carvings, which he left to his sons and grandsons. As the image depicts, there are many gifts of the sun in the form of light, heat, radio waves, sound, and radiations as yet undefined. With this information as to the massive amounts of energy being given to all beings in an equal manner all of the time, there was never any doubt as to the beneficence of the Creator who allowed him to live in such a blessed environment.

Thus he captured in images, which he designed, the blessings of Maat as seen in nature. For if the original intention of the creation of the universe was to freely give gifts of life and energy, then it followed that one must be at peace and live in harmonious order as made possible by nature. He understood that those who have gifts should give them just as the sun does. This philosophy became the foundation of his peaceful society.

Joyce: This sounds so simple and easy to understand. I can see why the sun disk would work as a symbol of the Amarna Experience. So you were saying that many travelers came to visit Egypt and saw the two cultures and wondered about them.

Revered Healer: One who came was the son of the ruler of India and he outlined for himself how the original teachings were carried on in Amarna as opposed to the declining thoughts elsewhere in Egypt. He left with the fervent intention to never do anything but the Highest Good, for he could see how the soul's endeavor to reach the Presence of God could be eclipsed by such errant thought as fear and doubt. He made contact with the Hathors who helped him to do great things in India.

So much good was done in so many ways in those days, that one wondered which culture was best, that of India or Egypt. In the middle of all of this cultural development, sat Amarna where the plants flowered in an extraordinary way, people lived to very old ages in perfect health, and babies prospered no matter how they were born.

With these two countries evolving peacefully with great prosperity, there was not much that could be said for those in between. Many of the warlike and poverty cultures were diminishing into feudal kingdoms ruled by cruel and fierce kings. The world populations who wanted peace were flocking to these two peaceful countries, which soon enjoyed a very diverse population with all of the advantages of their skills, tools, abilities, and diverse DNA.

One of those countries to lose much of their culture to the two giants of peace was Syria, which was soon planning to make war on Egypt. Since Egypt had never experienced much in the way of war, they were totally unprepared for what was about to happen. In Armana, however, the people knew how to welcome the warriors in peace and to feed them, heal them and educate them, while the other cities tried to defend themselves and defeat the invaders.

The effect of the Amarna approach was for the Syrians to see the benefits of the Amarna approach and to make peace. As a result, they learned many of the technological trades and skills of Egypt that would make them rich and healthy. The other Egyptian cities, seeing the effect, realized the difference between the old and new thought systems, seeing that to revert to the old teachings would have superior results. And thus even war was used to promote peace.

Thus, Amarna was no longer isolated as it had been at its founding, as everyone came and went, learning and gaining in their peace consciousness. The old pyramids were re-commissioned with the daily intentions for the Highest Good, and prosperity returned across Egypt. Thus the people of Amarna traveled around to the other cities and did great things for each of them, teaching and founding schools of enlightenment. For they, who had succeeded in opening their Higher Minds were indeed the teachers and leaders, just as in the old times. Eventually most of the people moved to other cities and even some of the stones from Amarna were used to pave the way for new ventures of peace elsewhere.

Joyce: So there was quite a contrast in the two ways of treating a warring invader. Interesting. It makes me think about karma. There is always an easy way and a hard way to progress to peace. Making war and maintaining a defensive mentality is the hard way and the way of Maat is the easy way. The way of Maat is always to give good and never harm. Thus those who came with the intention for conflict found that they could get much more of what they wanted by asking and could do it without bloodshed. As this was good for both populations, making even more good available to others, it was easy to change willingly from intending harm to intending good. Everybody wants good and if they can have it without war, so much the better. I would imagine that societies who exercise these principles would have so little grief and so much prosperity and happiness that they would never want to give it up. Sweet.

Revered Healer: There is much good to learn from these times and little that is bad, unless you think that giving up fear and grief and learning how to live in peace is bad. Indeed, always seeking the easy way for her beloved family, the Mother of the Revered Healer (reincarnated as Nefertiti) gave her best efforts to create great openings to the Hathors and thus empower such productive changes. Later in her life, one group of travelers who came from Western Africa made the acquaintance of the Great Mother and invited her to travel back with them to their homeland to found such a society for them. These were the early farmers and trades people of the Dogon. Never one to decline a request for Maat, Great Mother traveled with them, living with them for the rest of her life, teaching them all that she knew, especially making contact with the Hathors possible for them.

In Egypt, she was sorely missed. Her images in Egypt were erased because she was so sorely missed. But, as it was her choice to leave, they left her image blank until she would return again in etheric form as she had promised.

Joyce: So you say that the Great Mother actually left Egypt. That must have broken her heart because she had such a large and loving family. Tell me how and why she did that.

Revered Healer: How and why was not the question in her mind, but rather what kind of good could be done to raise once again, a totally pure culture in love with love as you are about to do today. If you were us, would you not grant her safe passage through all mountains, plains, and even waterways, so as to bring such a prize to the plains of Africa to do such a great work? Thus it was done and her efforts are still resident in the art, language, and society that live there today. Is that not the act of a truly great mother? Who would not want to accompany her, but her companions of ancient times? Yes, my dear, we traveled together on the long journey and never left each other's presence. And we are soon to repeat the same process in this lifetime.

Joyce: Oh my, what a great adventure. I'm glad that she didn't go alone. Sharing her reincarnated intention, I hope to find all of my beloved family returned in this lifetime to work together once again for the Highest Good.

Revered Healer: Coming and going, it's always a pleasure to be with you.

Now we have come to the story of ancient Egyptian writing with its unforgettable images. From ancient times, our powerful symbols had served as a form of story telling, but they did not constitute a written language. Later, the symbols were to be used in the construction of the language of the later pharaohs. More precisely, the Egyptian language was developed from the ancient symbols during the times of the pharaohs into a series of translatable languages developed over time. There were, in fact, many Egyptian languages. And so it is for the Egyptian scholars to decide which is the best way for a term to be understood for they are not all the same at all times. Many of the texts at the time reverted to old understandings that were very simple and even studied by children and easily understood. Other texts used quite elaborate systems of writing and depictions that are still in existence today, but do not mean the same as others, but which look similar. They are hard to read and decode without a thorough understanding of the history during the period in which they were used. To translate them properly, one must understand how the people thought about many of the realities of their lives at the time that the writings were made.

In short, some of these writings were very confusing mixtures of the old high truths and the declining beliefs. For example, there were some who thought that reincarnation was the result of magic spells chanted at the time of death. Others thought that the spells were meaningless and that it was the choice of the departed to choose for himself or herself what their next life would be. Thus a period of confusion followed in which no one was sure of which way Egyptian thought would go. However, there were always the old and true symbols such as Maat, Ka, and the Ankh, but even these were at times used for meanings other than their original ones. Therefore to decipher the hieroglyphs of this period is quite challenging.

As luck would have it, there was once again a visitor from China to appear with a group of pioneers who wanted to travel the world and found schools of higher thought everywhere they went. In seeking the wisdom of Egypt, he stayed for a long time and copied the original papyrus into the Chinese at the time. The visitor from China found the symbols too difficult to draw, so he simplified them using them in streamlined form as part of the Chinese language. Those writings are still in existence and will be made available to the scholars who ask to be directed to them. They will help scholars to decode the hieroglyphs of that period as well as to document the influence of Egyptian writing on the Chinese language.

Moreover, this man well understood the value of the term Maat and made it his way of living. With this intention, there was much good to be had by him and little harm, so Highest Good would always be his guide. On all occasions, he and his group let the Hathors be their advisors and much that was developed as science and invention came from those early attempts to spread civilization evenly and fairly all over the world. This man opened the Silk Road and fortified it with the beginnings of the Great Wall of China.

The Silk Road opened the world to the Mongolian Highlands and their warring tribes, who wanted to turn in their little ponies for Egyptian chariots. Their belief system required that none but the best be served to them as conquerors in tems of treasures, women, wine, and food. They considered themselves great conquerors, having the right to take what they wanted. Thus they were the cause of great harm. But they were not prepared for what they found in Egypt: The generally non-warring community of Egyptians had learned something of warfare before their arrival and had built up substantial armies.

The Egyptians defeated the invading Mongols, but then quickly educated them, healed them, and gave them all of the benefits of their society, including access to the Hathors. As a result, there were many of the Mongolians who would later return to China to become great kings with Highest Good on their minds.

They founded great societies and led the world in trade and exploration of vast areas of resources, all available to the ordinary citizen. In the end, there was much good and little harm and the world turned from war to peace.

Much of what is now modern India and Tibet was, in fact, a base of operations for an Indian army of missionaries so persuasive that they could turn the nations of the world into a world trade association. Much good and little harm caused the populations of the Earth to multiply and for the many wonders of the ancient world to be reproduced in many different ways and means.

Joyce: I am surprised to hear of the Mongolians in Egypt. That's a long way to come. Why did they make the effort?

Revered Healer: Their ways of making war needed testing against the greatest empires of the world, or so they thought. But the story of the spread of Highest Good goes even further.

Next we come to the differing cultures of the Native American Indians, the Mayans, and Bolivians of South America, all of whom were descendants of the refugees from the sinking Continent of Atlantis. These remnants of the fleeing Atlanteans founded cities in the Americas. One such city in the Andes was referred to as Tiahuanaco. It was near Lake Titicaca where great amounts of gold were discovered and often discarded in the great lake in hopes of contacting the Hathors as, at that time, their knowledge of the Hathors was only legendary. Therefore the lake had the reputation of being of great magic, for it never gave the contact that they sought. Something better was needed. Since a great society based upon the principles of the Highest Good was desired, the Hathors, although not in communication, were in great support. Soon word was sent to Amarna to find someone to help them to found such a society.

Thus the great one chosen by the Egyptians to do this was the great one who later called himself, Quetzalcoatl. He traveled from Egypt to South America by boat and overland trails. He was recognized when he arrived as he had very unusual abilities. For example, he was famous for being blind in one eye but still able to see through it, using mental viewing. He led his people through mountain passes unerringly with only the intention for the Highest Good as his guide. Using his etheric mental third eye, he knew that destiny had great help in store for him. In addition, his mate, who came with him from Egypt, was able to open many of the people to their own channel. As a people, they enjoyed the good advice that the Hathors had to give. The people were overjoyed and the Hathors made them aware of how to build monuments similar to those in Egypt, but of different design. They used massive stones, all lifted and moved with the help of the Hathors. Even today, we see much of the same amazing feats of engineering and records of long-lived people who enjoyed peace and happiness for lengthy periods of time. Their long history was one of mostly true belief, but sometimes they had periods of fear and greed and then returned again to revive the original principles. These people eventually became known as the Mayans.

Upon his passing, Quetzalcoatl left a promise to return to help them again. When the Spanish arrived thousands of years later, the local people incorrectly thought that they were greeting the family of the reborn Quetzalcoatl. And so the people who lived in peace and prosperity for centuries were to be greatly disappointed and tested by the invaders who were ironically also descendants of refugees from Atlantis. The Spanish came and saw the gold, taking what they could and leaving behind death, disease, fear, and panic as well as a strong desire to return to the days of peace. Thus there is resident in these countries even today, where the original seeds of peace were sown so long ago, as much will to succeed with peace as anywhere else on Earth.

To the far north, the Native American Indians of North America, who were descendants of refugees from Atlantis, were living a natural life of hunting, sitting around campfires, inter tribal trade, and loving their families according to tradition. In their tribes, none but the finest of food and resources were made available to the least able or oldest of the tribe, thus the Highest Good was at work. Their system of government was much more of a nature religion, in which many of the decisions were made through the use of signs provided by weather, animals, and events. It tended toward superstition, but was altogether a wholesome way to live.

They prospered and lived in family tribes for generations, traveling from the East to the midlands and even farther west where the plains Indians met up with some from the tribes from the south who were descendants of the Atlantean/Mayan tribes of Central America. These two cultures were surprisingly similar and so they intermingled easily and formed the basis of the culture of the American Southwest Indian community. These people worshiped only the god of nature and communed with their ancestors, but surprisingly not the star beings. Instead, an etheric form of the Christ Consciousness contacted them just as he had Akhenaten, asking them to observe the principles of the Highest Good in all of their relationships. They did this, but the society was patriarchal and ritualistic and few had the idea of contacting the spirit realms on their own right. A frequent drawing of this being has been found on rock drawings. He is shown as a huge 12-foot man with square shoulders, a small head, and tiny arms. These are images that they were able to capture, not necessarily as he intended to appear to them.

Drawing of American Indian vision of the Christ Consciousness

We find these native tribes lived in close harmony with nature until the white settlers came to farm the land and herd animals across the arid dry lands. Under such a massive invasion, there was a feeling of non-support among the tribes as the Native Americans were helpless against the more powerful weapons, tools, and numbers of well-organized white soldiers. The Native Americans' way of life declined as they languished for quite some time turning from peace to warfare and back again to peace. Eventually their fate was to be banished to reservations as helpless dependents of the federal government. They, too, have a great desire to return to their old traditions as well as to contribute their cultural teachings to finding a new way for the world to live in peace.

With so many examples of how the seed of peace can grow in so many ways, wherever it is planted, it makes the process of peace seem all the more attractive.

That now brings us to the gathering of the returnees who are finding that peace is on their minds in a new way these days. We would like to discuss some methods of resurrecting the old in a new way. We would not say that modern conditions of fear and grief have irretrievably burdened us with disease, crime, terrorism, and great natural disasters. Rather, we find much that is good and we only desire to correct the bad.

We would like to demonstrate that all aspects of the destructive work of fear comes through the Human Aura and resides there, spreading from consciousness to consciousness through mass media, physical contact and disastrous forecasting. Once fear is resident in the auras of generation after generation of people, it is recorded as factual history where it is taught and reinforced, appearing to be even more irreversible. Thus one fear creates another and so forth with no reprieve. And so the question to consider is how could so many have come to believe that a civilization like ancient Egypt and Amarna and the others actually existed in peace for so long? Thus the interest in archeology is high today and will get more intense when verification of these readings is sought.

But of much more effect will be the example of intentional communities devoted to peaceful, Earth-friendly lifestyles, formed not just as experiments but also to be residential places of peace for the world to draw from to heal from fear. With this in mind, those who have never experienced success are the ones most determined to have it. Thus these intentional communities could be started in areas were the poor, discomforted, disadvantaged, and even drug addicted are found. Indeed Native American Indian reservations are ideal, for these people have suffered the most extreme form of Highest Good reversal including the effects of alcoholism, drug abuse, family breakups, and even gambling. However, since they have been deemed the independent nations that they are, they are free to revive a culture of their own choosing. As soon as they make that choice and make it known to the rulers at hand and include women and children in all that is good, there is much good that can be had for their nations.

As well, rural communities that are far from cities, but have the work ethic and sense of community that a rural culture demands will find a ready supply of those who wish to improve their land and farming practices to be free of the conglomerates which prohibit the use of seeds other than their own. Such community efforts can be economically feasible should the whole community come to the support of the idea that viable farming needs to be local. Indeed, even in the cities, there are to be found the beginnings of rural farming culture in the remains of demolished ruined buildings leaving empty lots. Many of the small cultural centers and schools have offered their help to educate children to the values of self grown food and to eradicate the illnesses of processed foods shipped too far to be nutritious any longer.

This will be true for the indigenous Indians of other countries as well, who have found that their native cultures have remnants of the old truths, but need to be rid of cruel and limiting superstitions that have accumulated through fear and prejudice. Many of the traditional herbal and ceremonial healings practices are of great value and can be incorporated into new practices even in clean sterile environments such as clinics and hospitals.

As for the restoration of the soil to full fertility without fertilizers and chemicals, there are methods that will be made available from spirit contact that will revolutionize the growing of food. What is so needed for the elongation of the human life and the rebuilding of the body to its original DNA code of perfection is partly good food, but mostly the reconnection with the nourishment of the blue light of the next dimensions through the human aura. Only the reduction of fear will accomplish this.

As for the medical and social services, there are indeed those who labor long and hard to be a friend to the needy, but are not well supported by general society. Neither do they need to give resources without a return. Rather the goal of returning people to their independence and capabilities to help others is the leavening of even more resources. Therefore these social services do well when they demand that homes be cleaned up and children sent to good schools in drug-free environments. Thus we have those raised to be competent, saying to us: "Thank you, you have made me whole and therefore I know how to make others whole as well. So let me do it, for I know both the lack and the abundance of good and am thereby most capable of returning much more than was given to me."

As far as social institutions are concerned, there is none more important than the Higher Mind to be in full care of its lesser cousin, the Conscious Mind. Therefore we propose that before anything else can be taught to anyone, there is the need for all involved to be at peace. For peace consciousness is the one and only way to be truly educated. With peace we enter into a Consciousness transfer that far exceeds what the Conscious Mind can do alone. Therefore, we shall be learning to defeat the grief and fears of the Conscious Mind and thus open to Higher Consciousness. We should do all of our work with the intention for the Highest Good, whether it is to research a potshard or to sell a new cell phone. Thus it starts and ends with peace and thus it will succeed.

But in doing our work and professions, do we also need the Hathors to sort out for us, once again, how to be sure that our actions have no harm? We can ask the Hathors for solutions that make no mistakes as far as science and industry is concerned, and thus does no harm to the environment or individuals, using methods so safe and efficient that none can complain. As many of these solutions come from the minds of inventors, would we not need to provide a safe and protected environment for inventors of the products of Highest Good to prosper, as Nicolas Tesla so needed? He succeeded to give us great gifts of the use of electricity, but he died an impoverished, lonely man in grief. How would a pharaoh be judged if he allowed those in his care to be mistreated and then sent home hungry to die alone?

For such occurrences to be avoided, there is much to be considered by those who care enough about peace to study it, make it and be it. Thus we find that although the Constitution of the United States of America guarantees everyone the right to pursue their happiness by means of the Highest Good, there is great harm in deeds done with an intention fostered by greed and abuse. Thus we find that those in charge of great wealth have a responsibility to distribute it wisely and fairly for the common good. As it was their blessing to have had the opportunity to gain the wealth in the first place, it is also their responsibility to do something with the wealth to help the whole society. When this is widely supported from the heart, the stock market will no longer swing wildly and much peace and prosperity will result.

Can those wandering the streets homeless and sick be cared for with respect and given responsibility to be participants of society once again? Would that the remnants of the dignity of the mentally ill be given one small dose of love and concern as to be set free by means of hypnotically induced euphoria, a great gift of the Hathors, ready to be given at any time to those who request it?

There is so much to be had with so little effort that none can complain, but to be grace givers of this magnitude, one must begin by sitting in the sunny window and facing one's fears and grief. And being so healed and made happy, one may leave, free in mind and soul, to be peace givers. Thus we return once more to the time in Egypt's past when this same resurrection was well accomplished, so as to show a new way of making peace.

Chapter Four:
As Amarna Was, So Goes the Future

Revered Healer: As Amarna was dug deep into the sands of time, we find that there is another feature of the site as yet undiscovered, but it soon will be. Those who wished to visit with the star beings on a nightly basis needed a sheltered environment from which to view the star Sirius and no other. Thus there is to be found among the site builder's remains, the drawings of a deep tunnel that was aligned toward Sirius whenever it appeared on the horizon, which was about every seventy days. For when Sirius was below the horizon, there was little hope to contact the beings, or so it seemed at the time.

As the relationship between the Egyptians and the star beings developed, there were many of the spirit kind who came to the assistance of those who wished to be friends all of the time. Therefore, arrangements were being made so that constant contact could be maintained. Thus we come to the sending of the great Christ Consciousness to establish a much-needed code of conduct for those to follow who have returned to be peacemakers once again. We think of them as Reunioners. In living in peace with each other as he taught, Christ's followers enjoyed reliable passage between the dimensions. Indeed the final words of Christ as recorded in the Gospels are: "I am the way, the truth, and the light. For this there is needed much peace in your heart. Therefore, treat your brother as yourselves and make peace in all aspects of your lives and I will be there with you to assure that your efforts are not wasted. For with the assistance that I will provide, there is no fail to the system of peace."

Thus the nature of this great man's life was not to be found so much in the sacrifice of his death, but in the message of his life. For this to be made clear, we must review much that has been lost regarding the events preceding his death and indeed during his life. These things need to be understood, for their significance is at hand. Indeed, his return is at hand. For the first time that he came in human form, he entered through the portal of birth, but today he returns through the portals of dimensional spiritual travel, which he himself opened and manages for our use.

Thus we return once more to the Bible in which are described the trials and tribulations of the Egyptian prince named Moses, once a Hebrew child left to be found by a Egyptian princess. In this story, there is also a great mother who, with no concern for her son's safety, followed the instructions from above and floated a basket containing her son on the river in the area where the princess would find it. When the princess, who had not had children of her own, found the basket with a beautiful baby boy, she was prompted to adopt the lost child as her own and make him a prince of Egypt. Ironically, we find that both women had the same birthdates and had been switched at birth (as was not uncommon in those days). Thus the one who thought herself high born was of the common people and the one who considered herself low born one was indeed the true princess giving her son to his true destiny.

It was with such fateful beginnings in life that the drama of the two women and the one son collide in a miscarriage of justice. For Moses, being a wise man with a kind heart, acted to prevent the death of a lowly worker at the risk of an Egyptian. Being accused of turning against one of his own kind, he would, by law, have to be sent away to live alone without either family. And so he left Egypt walking alone into the desert wilderness with only his staff and his belief in himself as a good man.

While wandering the wilderness in dire loneliness, however, Moses made contact with Higher Mind and found his own version of the Presence of God. And with that contact, he opened his heart to being loved and cared for by his Higher Mind and found his own peace and contentment. He asked for and received help with all of his daily problems. He was led to find a good wife and become a valued member of her family. He was shown a way to make a living as a herdsman and shown a mountain to retreat to for long conversations with his spirit. It was from these conversations that he was to later record the commandments to be of the Highest Good. With this, the man born to be a Jew, raised to be a prince, and living as a sheep herder raises his consciousness such that he cannot but find his wife beautiful, his children a blessing, and his simple life a joy. But when he is commanded to reenter Egypt to have discourse with the rulers who had sent him away, including the women who were his mothers, he died a thousand deaths.

Imagine him, a wanted man, walking into the Pharaoh's court to ask for the right to lead the common people away. What man would he prove to be, but the one to take an abused people and lead them through the desert with nothing there to sustain them but sand, sun, and dew? With his own Higher Mind to guide him through the difficulties, however, he managed to give an emerging new nation a trial and error existence in which to hone their belief in the Highest Good and no other. How like the experience of Amarna is the story of this man's life? How like a small boy in the far future that teaches the priests in the temple what his Father's house is all about?

Once Moses had determined that his God was good and would lead him in a good direction, his trust opened the way for many more to believe the same. The stories of the wanderings in the desert tell many wonderful examples of overcoming doubt and building trust in the God who promised to lead them to a peaceful place to live. Indeed Moses and his people laid the foundation for the opening that Christ later created. In fact, many souls have lived many lifetimes with the desire to participate in the intentions of peace that the Christ Consciousness has for this beautiful planet. We bring you this series of books to illustrate that the history of the Earth is full of those who made peace a priority in order to create conditions for it to flourish. All encountered doubt, fear, and want, but ultimately found success. Each time another came to pursue the same intention, the seed of peace advanced.

How can we use the experience of Amarna and Moses today? Have we noticed that there are many conditions that need to be in place for the reunion between the two minds, the Conscious and the Higher, to be successful? First there is the need for setbacks, demise, and abuse to be in recent memory so that those who wish peace have a great enough desire for it to persevere through wearing down the function of the fearful Conscious Mind in all levels of society. Thus the first condition is a great need followed by a great desire.

The second condition is the intention for the Highest Good followed by an opening to the Higher Mind. We offer this so that the Amarna experience can be properly understood. If it is, then the method that was given by Christ Himself and those of his compatriots, who risked their lives to be present at just the right time to perform the Highest Good, can be understood as well.

There is the leverage of the Highest Good to be considered. For if one wants to lift a great weight to a good height, it must have a long lever placed at a strategic point in time and place. In this case, that place is within one's own mind. When one says to oneself *I am unable to overcome the fears that life is too heavy a weight to lift alone*, one finds the greatest leverage. At that moment of clarity, one is open to help from the Higher Mind, which comes flooding in. Nothing is ever the same again. Many, like Moses and Akhenaten, have come for this experience and to lead others through it as well.

Thus there is great cause for recognition among the community of Reunioners returned from prior lives and for them to enjoy their company together. Some will do their service as solitary bringers of peace and others will be in the limelight and forefront of open discussion. All should be supported equally. There are also those, however, whose life path it is to be in the midst of seemingly disastrous change and reversals of fortunes, beliefs, and experiences. We find that these have a seemingly contrary kind of life, but are also to be supported.

Thus we come to the story of Cleopatra, who was chosen to serve as queen of a dying country. She rose to the occasion and did her best, even if to no avail. In the end she abdicated the rule of Egypt through death only to return again at this time. In suffering so much trial by defeat, she should be entitled to a good and long-lasting life this time around. In doing so, she has the chance to review the evidence as to how to understand and revive the best of Egypt and to discard the useless parts as remnants of Conscious Mind thinking of long ago. For not all that existed in Egypt was sacred, but that which was needs to be uncovered, documented, and researched to the satisfaction of the seekers of truth.

For the worldwide repercussions of what Cleopatra did in the last century before Christ was a miraculous defeat of her own self for the benefit of a new beginning that we can now make two thousand years later. And for that she shall be honored at last.

And so she is now in reincarnated form and shall open the Hall of Records beneath the paw of the Sphinx, making good on Cayce's dream. For In 1937, Edgar Cayce dreamed that the tablets recording the history of the Highest Good long hidden in a secret chamber under the paw of the Sphinx had been discovered and were sent to his home along with a mummy in a sarcophagus. While he was studying the tablets, the mummy began to awake and stood up, shaking off the old paint and plaster revealing a vibrant young woman. She worked with Cayce to translate the tablets, which began to tell the history of Egypt up to the Amarna period in which the tablets were buried. The tablets verified much of what the Cayce readings had said about Egyptian history and its influence on the cultures of the world. They included three tablets from the time of Cleopatra with Roman Numerals on them. Cleopatra had opened the chamber in her time as Queen and consulted them about her role and duty to Egypt. She returned the older tablets along with three new ones that she wrote and signed with her insignia to the chamber under the Sphinx and sealed them with the intention for the Highest Good. And thus Cayce's dream ended without finishing the translations. Reborn today, she was given the privilege to research them again and to bring Egypt back to the full knowledge of the foundations of its glory and her role in founding the modern plan for peace.

Thus it is that none who made the intention for the Highest Good will ever be disappointed in the eventual outcome. And so we return once more to the story of Amarna to view a way for the current population of the world to empower its peaceful future.

Chapter Five:
Seeds of Amarna Sown Once Again

Revered Healer: In the beginning of the day that leveled the twin towers of the New York Trade Center, there was a softly spoken promise made by many who were left behind to grieve their losses, to end such acts of hate and violence. In that brief moment so much harm was done, that the shock and awe consummated in a firm determination that it should never happen again to any nation on Earth. With that determination, many nations gathered together, not just to track down the criminals and bring them to justice, but also to acknowledge and remedy the causes for the crime.

Thus, there has been much interest in the relief of the poor in the Middle East from which much terrorism arose. In these countries there is much need for the equalization of the classes as well as for the welfare of women and children. Many men are conscripted for war without their consent and made to conform to practices abhorrent to their beliefs. Such things are not in the Highest Good and need to be remedied, but not with violence. Rather a new Amarna approach needs to be worked out so that all can participate in the good of an expanding world economy. Let us consider what happened next in Amarna, once the needs of the people had been satisfied and sufficient education and protection of health had been in place for a long time.

In this segment of Egypt's history, there were territories, like modern states, that represented a geographical area with special interests. Representatives of these territories would meet regularly in a council to do business on behalf of the good of all. To be a member of this advisory council, it was necessary for one to have knowledge of the needs of the people and to intend the good of all. When all were represented in the kind of way that would be effective for the entire region, some decisions could be made such as where caravan routes could be set for the bringing of certain goods and information that would help all to prosper. Protection for travelers and business people was arranged, as well as standards for honest and fair business transactions. And with this being done, the members of the advisory council returned to their towns with outlines of what had been recommended.

If agreeable to all, then the representatives were sent back to the council to enact a form of legislation, which was posted on carved stones in several languages at junctures of roads, towns, and ports. All could be advised about the facilities available, the rules that would apply, and who was responsible for their safe passage. It was a simple system, but all who heeded the regulations passed without fear and all enjoyed the best outcome because the interests of the traders were considered as well as those of the local people.

During this time, there was a significant difference between a foreign trader and a local dealer in goods and services. A trader was a foreigner and relatively unknown, but a dealer was a local person whose reputation was generally known. Thus, the business economy operated on the trust that was built over time by those who practiced the intention for the Highest Good in the local area. This trust was viewed as the major way in which the principle of the Highest Good was enacted in business. Thus we come to the part of the story when Amarna was big enough and strong enough in terms of both needs and resources to be admitted into the territory council and thus have a carved stone erected by its road.

In those days, a road was considered to be anything from a dirt path made by wild donkeys going to watering holes, to a paved road made of stones or brick. Most families had the habit of throwing their garbage into a pit and then mixing it up into a slop to be put into molds for the making of bricks. Thus the economy walked on its own trash. Such were the thought processes that worked to the benefit of all, including the environment in which they lived.

When under consideration for participation in the territorial council, a town had to meet certain standards in terms of the common good. These included the condition of their trash dumps, fertility of their fields, upkeep of their wells, roads, places of prayer, schooling methods, and even the care and condition of their mothers as they were responsible for raising good citizens who could work and buy goods. By means of these standards, the council was composed of those practicing the first and best rule of law; no harm and lots of good as outlined in the principle of the Highest Good. Since traders and local dealers had much to gain by good conduct of business, and much to lose by poor practices, they gladly complied with honest and fair business practices. There was little need for a justice system, because the consequences of bad intentions were obvious and effective. Since the community was small and all talked to each other, they compared notes as to their business experiences and no one would buy from someone who gave harm.

The justice system consisted of tribunals or places to hear complaints and to seek a solution. Those who were accused of a crime or misdemeanor were called to account by the tribunals for their actions. This accounting was not as much for the purpose of blame and punishment as for compensation. For example, someone might rob a family of their milk. This person would be told to buy the same quantity of milk and give it back to the family. Thus it became well known that none who were harmed would be harmed again, as long as the tribunal heard their cause with honesty.

To insure honesty, the accused was trusted to the care of the world's best authority on lying and cheating, namely parents. It might sound strange, but if a person lied to the tribunal, their parents were called to rename their errant children in two names. The first was their birth names and the second as a liar. Thus it was recorded in normal conversation, "so and so, the liar" was coming and none would trust them until the name had been removed through honesty and complete compensation for any harm done.

Thus the entire system was simple and inexpensive in terms of time and stress. Much depended on the integrity of the town to enforce through its own opinion of itself being a good town in which to live and do business. No one wanted to be known as a bad place to live, thus standards were maintained for the common good. Thus we come to the issues facing modern society.

There is a main agency of federal government in most countries that could be held to certain standards such as human rights and the use of resources for the common good by the larger council of countries. In fact such a council of countries already does exist and is functioning as the United Nations. It is the right and responsibility of participating countries to refuse to engage in trade with those who do not participate to standard unless they ask for help with their problems. Is not this the function of sanctions? Such things can and are enacted, but are not yet well supported by the whole community of countries. In some cases, countries do not want fair trade practices as they, themselves, practice human and environmental abuse. Thus there are observer organizations that report in a verifiable manner to the world, the conditions present in all countries, including those of environmental and human rights practices. While having established so much that is good, it is certain that some non-participants in the common good principles have had the advantage of vast amounts of natural resources so needed by the rest of the world that their abuse is too often overlooked and thus practiced freely.

It would be good in so many ways, that the use of the open channel to the Hathors be offered and available to those countries wishing to reduce their dependence upon resources from countries engaging in abuse. Thus we find that these fine friends of the spirit realm, the Hathors, are looking for cooperating engineers, inventors, and scientists to whom they can give very valuable insights that would allow economic independence of such depleting resources. Their only requirement is to apply as a Beloved One, on behalf of other Beloved Ones and to request help that would assure the Highest Good for all. Should anyone apply—even abusing countries – it would be given, starting with advice on how to clean up their own problems first. Thus whoever applies for such help will be given the advice that is best for their conditions at the time. Others who apply later will be given advice for conditions at that later time. None will be denied unless their intention is a perverse one.

In such a simple manner, much good can be done and since the Hathors offer an etheric source of advice, the information is guaranteed to be simple, easy, and harmless, giving so much good to the world that no one would think of going anywhere else for advice or help. In addition, all good advice would be shared with all as soon as is feasible such as on the Internet. For the Highest Good cannot be hoarded. To keep it flowing, it must be shared with all.

After Earth-friendly and peace-enhancing inventions and methods have been practiced for a long time, the economies of the world will gradually equalize until everyone will have a share in the prosperity of such peaceful living. Since practices such as terrorism would significantly jeopardize such commerce, all efforts necessary would be enacted to prevent the causes or outbreaks of them. That would include preventing the production and selling of illegal drugs, certain weapons, and even religious practices promoting violence as if it were a spiritual goal. With violence effectively eliminated, there is nowhere in the world where one could go and not expect to be treated as a valued customer, vendor, and fellow traveler.

With this in place, there is much to be gained by the proper nourishment of babies and children with their mother's milk and healthy food without food additives. Thus, support and advice about the common practice of nursing babies, local farmers' markets, home gardens, and natural food products will be offered, as would be expected by the Highest Good.

Indeed many of the medical woes of the populace would cease as the pressures to work in dangerous areas and to produce more income than is comfortable to earn are eliminated. With a modest lifestyle reducing stress, families will need a wide variety of living arrangements. These may range from communal homes with common sanitary systems and general participation in local work, to palatial estates much of which would be open to the public as gardens, museums, schools of creative arts, and public meeting rooms. Those who have earned much will begin to want to say: "Take some of mine, for I have much to give. For if I give, I have much more to receive." The worst condition for anyone is to be so satiated with luxury and indolence that one cannot be content and happy.

For all of this housing to be made simple, efficient, low cost, and available to all, it will be made of materials that conduct solar energy. The internal temperature will be largely controlled by a roofing system that either lets in cold air and prohibits warm, or holds in heat and prohibits cold. With such housing, no large machines will be needed for heat or cooling. Electricity generated from simple solar cells can be installed to produce low cost, local electricity to supplement passive heating and cooling as well as to power reduced-voltage tools and equipment. There will, however, still be a need for the transmission systems of large amounts of power for certain high voltage functions as well as a need to provide for those on the dark side of the rotation of the Earth. But the generation of that power will be from natural sources, not the burning of fossil fuels. All of this is possible with a little engineering, planning and redesign of devices. Suggestions will be given aplenty from the etheric sources of the universe.

And so we end this chapter with the same greeting that the Hathors, gave to the citizens of Amarna: "Pleased to meet you. What needs may we help you with that will lead to peace? Give us a jingle. It doesn't take a star chart to find us anymore. We are as near as a wish list in the hands of a Higher Mind thinker"

Chapter Six:
If Walls Could Speak

Revered Healer: Once one has an idea of how the Amarna Experience clarifies how to proceed on the path to peace, one only has to let the walls speak to see how the story ended for those in Amarna and to appreciate how it will work in modern times.

Therefore, we return to the Amarna of ancient times and listen to the walls of the Great Hall and temple that was the focus of their activities and see what is going on. This Great Hall had been designed by suggestions from the Hathors and, being a rectangle consisting of an outer series of rooms under roof, it had an inner courtyard with temporary stalls as would be suited for a farmer's market.

At the time of the recording of the great stellea of congratulations on becoming a member of the territory council, there were many citizens who had come to the first meeting room on the right to negotiate their rights to be licensed entrepreneurs. At that time, they had to prove that they promoted their businesses in fairness to both vendors and customers because it followed that if too many complaints were made, their licenses would be revoked until they returned to their senses. Being that people did not want to be mistreated, they always looked for the sign of the license before doing business.

Many who had goods, produce, and wares to sell looked for the most advantageous places in the central marketplace so as to realize a good return on their efforts. Thus the best-priced vendor was given the best spot and the highest priced the least. In the market place, there was no relief from the hot sun, so the money charged for the licenses was used for maintaining the canopy that protected produce and enticed customers with the shade.

The use of apprenticeships was promoted to allow youngsters growing up to learn from the best practitioners. Those who wanted the low cost labor of an apprentice had to apply showing that their expertise was high and the treatment practices good. On tomb walls, a painting still remains as an example of trade groups.

Drawing of trade group dealing in cattle.

This is a portrait of several people walking in line carrying a long stick of some type of measuring material such as metal or wood. The measuring rod would be carried on their shoulders showing that each intends to hold up the standards of work and trade. The insignia of the trade would be on each end of the rod. In the case of butchers, dairymen, and herders, the heads of cattle would be placed at each end. It was not to say that only these few people were ever licensed, but that those who were, accepted the responsibility to measure up to the standards.

In the next room of the hall, there were the family practitioners of health services who were constantly diagnosing illnesses in terms of their causes, not necessarily cures. If one were wise enough to partake of the removal of the root causes of disease, finding the root cause and eliminating it would be sufficient treatment. For the others, there were those, empowered by long practice, to be pullers of teeth, setters of broken arms, and drillers of holes in craniums. The use of music was perhaps the easiest form of healing. Many instruments were used and it was always the intention of the healer/musician to contact the Higher Mind for the tones, melodies, and harmonies that best suited the healing intended. For those desiring to use their Higher Minds to cure health problems through mental seeing, they could attend the practice session of their local channeler from the Blue Dimension. These channelers offered the energetic cure, and also taught one how do make the connection to the Blue Dimension for oneself.

On these walls of the healing rooms, one would see a blue figure signifying the use of the energy of the Blue Dimension, holding the assortment of tools of herbs, oils, incense, a scalpel, a flute, and a dijed. The dijed looks like a pillar with several rings ascending from bottom to top. As the client told of the progress of the illness, the healer would show how each event in the life of the client was a progressive demonstration of how to heal the illness through increased understanding. When the conversation was complete, the client could leave with the understanding of how the events were designed to give the Highest Good, much like reading signs in other cultures. Thus they would know how to respond to instructions for their continued health. It was a form of health counseling.

The next room was devoted to the considerable use of acupuncture, which was begun in Egypt and carried to China by a monk in charge of the health care of his monastery. The Egyptians began the practice as a way to encourage the opening to channel. They were taught by the star beings that the pores of the skin were ideal places to place small needles so as to make a connection between the skin and the Higher Mind in the aura. Initially such knowledge was mainly used for opening to Higher Mind, but later was found to be of much use for health as well. On these walls, one would see a figure with the head of Anubis, the jackal, dissecting a body. This figure alone was considered dedicated enough to the highest good to have successfully studied the anatomy of the body and to practice the needle healing.

Annubis healer working on a body

Being completely immune to all diseases and fully able to work would require personal cleanliness; so young maidens performed the service of giving baths. They would scrub the skin, scalp, nails, and the nostrils, and then do a full body massage using oils and flower scents. Therefore the walls in their room were decorated with their images in clear, linen veils holding jars of oil and flowers.

Maidens doing body cleansing and playing healing music

If all of these fail to create health, then there were both the funeral emporiums and the tax takers who prepared a body for burial and made sure that the distribution of goods and responsibilities was fairly done, charging the family a fee before a person could officially be called dead. If their affairs were not cleared up to the satisfaction of the death tax takers, then the funeral processes could not be started which were of great importance in the society. The fees were used to pay workers to convert trash into bricks for the roadways. On the walls of the undertakers, you might see portraits of the funerary gods such as Horus, Isis, or Thoth carrying the remains of the deceased in jars so as to open their passage to the Higher Dimensions.

Joyce: After reading about the Amarna Experience, I am flooded with questions about how these practices can be applied to modern life. And since I seem to be the first one who is interested, would you explain it to me in terms of my experience? After all, I am the one who showed up for the experience, asked for it, did all of the preliminary exercises and studies and am the first to try it out. It is my life path to seek a viable way for peace to be given a firm foundation and good start in the next century. Secondly, since Dear Reader is still with me reading this in peace, and so deserves the same opportunity.

This time, I'm not so interested in the why of this whole thing because I can clearly see that its purpose is so good that it doesn't need to be questioned. Neither do I see any reason to be anything but joyful about what might be given next. So, I leap ahead with happy curiosity in my heart to say: Peaceful One, please explain to us all, how did the people of Amarna do all of this?

Peaceful One: Shall we not go back to the very beginning for you, in which you attempted to sort through the fears of the Conscious Mind and the wisdom of the Higher Mind? This was also the first step for the people of Amarna. It was all done through the use of channeled information and everyone was encouraged to develop a strong and open channel and to ask for the Highest Good. Indeed, their channel was often their primary tool for earning their living.

Joyce: Interesting. I see what you mean and I would evaluate it as excellent way to get such strong advice as to cure people of illnesses. However, I remember that it took a lot of concentration to separate Higher Mind out from the confusing advice of other sources, including my own fears. Then I had to get it so clear in my mind and heart that the many ways in which it has manifested good could be so clearly seen that doubt would virtually disappear. This would not have been easy for someone to learn. They must have had a peaceful environment in which to live to make it easy and reliable.

Peaceful One: Yes, they did. They used the watery environment of a pool with lotus plants for that purpose. However, all of the rest of the rules for a clear channel also applied. Just to clarify, remember that it has been our suggestion from the first that if one continues in fear, greed, or grief of any kind, that they will not be kindly treated by Karma, even if at first it might seem so. Then we said that to be kindly treated, that the first thing that one needs to do is to treat oneself kindly by being at rest when rest is due and avoiding additional stress and effort in the wrong direction. Lastly, did we not say that to be at peace requires that the participants in the transactions all be committed to the same goal? Thus in saying this, there is really nothing else to be said that is not kind and generous. Is that not a good summary of our relationship? It is the same between a health practitioners and the client.

Joyce: Yes, so it is. So let me summarize, if I am not at peace, then I should do nothing. If the other participant is not at peace, then I should ask the other to return to peace, send him or her away until they are or find another who is. Is that a short and sweet summary of how this all works?

Peaceful One: Yes, and the same is true with any solution or action including healing work with one who is in need. In short, no solution that does not contain 100 percent peace will succeed. In addition, a solution that has some parties only partially committed to peace will ultimately fail. Therefore, look for participants who have suffered the loss of their self-definition. They are incapable of being a controller of things, manipulating for their own good at the cost of others because they have failed so completely as the Conscious Mind would see it. Thus, the possibility for peace is evident, ready and capable of doing great things. Those who are humble, flexible, and only want peace are the best participants in any relationship including a healing one. Therefore, often the healers were those who had overcome disease themselves.

The same principles applied to all work and trades. Did you not see that in Amarna only those who had demonstrated their dedication to meeting the standard of their industry, trade, or family relations were admitted to the field of business transactions? Thus the trustfulness of the business community was such that none would dare to be dislodged for any reason. This trust came from the peaceful intentions. It is this feature of the Amarna experience that we wish to highlight for this part of the discussion. And so we will continue with yet another part of the story of Amarna and compare it to the experience of the U.S.A.

Being part of the community of territories was not thought of as a united kingdom or a federal government, which had control of any of the smaller towns. Rather, the council only served to provide for the common good on issues such as securing trade routes, the common rules of fair trade, and reliable communications between entities. As a comparison to the U.S.A., one might allow that the founding fathers intended that the federal government be of such service for the common good and not interfere with the states' production of good will to all of its citizens. However as the history of the United States unfolds with the expansion of an economy based upon slavery, the Highest Good was not being enjoyed by all who lived there, therefore a reversal event was set in motion, namely the Civil War.

A reversal is often thought of as a setback but, for this understanding, we would like to think of it as an unwinding of a thread of thought that was counter productive to the common good, so that it can rewind in a better way. Once this rewinding of the bad is accomplished (even with the loss of life) there is the need to found a new organization to spin it in the right direction. Continuing with this example, during the reformation of the new government after the Civil War, much that was good was built from the destruction. All parties were free to gather up the counterproductive tendencies and to rewind them in a better direction. We saw a series of such activities continuing well into the 1950's in which the meaning of freedom further unfolded. The true test of such freedom between whites and blacks is the successful election of a black man to the presidency. It is in this freedom that peace can be founded.

However, the adjustments for the Highest Good are not limited to the issues of race. Indeed they extend to financial concerns. When it was recently found that the financial institutions such as banks, investment houses, and the like had been participating in fraud and not doing the Highest Good in all manner of doing business, these were prohibited from participating in the future economy until complete restructuring was completed. It needed to start with the right intention, so no one will be in jeopardy of losing money for the wrong reason. Thus economic downturns have been as destructive as could be expected, but yet good has come of it. Such events arouse the general public to invest their funds only in companies well-founded in the Highest Good. Although the United States was founded upon the intention for the Highest Good, it needed several reversal events to happen in order to be certain that all who read history could see and appreciate what it means to be free to pursue one's own happiness. Much good has come from this history and, with a few more adjustments of the milder kind, a peace revival is possible that will infect the rest of the world's countries.

In Amarna, much the same transpired from time to time. There was little warfare, as the memory of the historical records of how well the reverse intentions created death and destruction were well advertised. The few battles, prisoners, slaughters, etc., depicted upon walls, stones, and papyrus, were mostly renditions of the potential effects of being in reverse and were placed there for the public service of saying: "No thanks, not for us." Most of them show a great being taking large steps to avoid such things by chopping of the head knots of hair or even heads of thought as to the wisdom of acting on destructive intentions. Even the castration scenes were to remind others that their children were in jeopardy of never being born. For if they proceeded in negative intentions, no one would marry them or carry their offspring with such intentions, as to do so brought bad consequences. Thus the stone carvings and wall murals were to portray the basic rules of the road for being in relationship with the Egyptians or indeed anyone, including animals, nature or the stars. Thus if you see depictions of animals with no heads, no tails, or strange combinations, it was a way to say that such distortions of seeing a blessed one deprived of their parts without their full consent was not permitted in the community.

Dearest Joyce, to relate it to your divorces and relationship issues, let's say that the marriage contract is one of the most sacred ones of your community as it means that children will be born and must bear the consequences of the actions of their parents. Innocent children being at risk, we find that if one party is found to be in the reverse intentions, they should proceed in another direction in peace. It is not that marriage is a disposable event in your or anyone's life, but a marriage, especially with children, must be founded in peace to be successful. Thus each divorce was given and received in peace with as much understanding as is possible. Thus the solitude following each divorce has granted you the best of outcomes, which is to never again look at the outward circumstances of a partner, but rather to expect to receive exactly what they intend and nothing more or less. You are resolved to let their track record, so to speak, speak for itself. With this to be such a calming outcome, one might even say that it has grief relief written all over it, for nothing less would ever be presented to you, being so sound in your intention to be at peace.

Joyce: This is an interesting way to look at my life. I realize that the commitment to be parents and a partner in a lifelong love creates a series of openings to face one's own challenges and to respond with good so as to do good for the whole family. Some couples continue on for their entire lives growing ever more beautiful from the marriage relationship. Other couples can come only so far before retreating in fear of changing their minds about themselves. So what does that say about modern marriage practices?

Peaceful One: As one may surmise, for a society to be at peace, there must be a period of long association before a marriage in which one who knows oneself to be well intentioned, finds the other to be so and all else being good and attractive, that the marriage can proceed in peace. And then when the going gets difficult and conflicts, discord, and anger arise, others in the family come forward to offer respite, advice and encouragement. It is with such support that one continues to open to better and better ways to be in the business of being married, so to speak.

Joyce: This seems like a very practical way to look at marriage and relationships. Humans are certainly not perfect, but if two people are committed to using their relationship to continue to open and unfold to the Highest Good, then it can be a vehicle of Enlightenment. But it would also make sense that some stop along the way and take a break or even bail out, hopefully leaving their partner in peace. That doesn't mean that either can't continue on and even make new relationships, but their history would speak for itself.

Peaceful One: Yes, such was everyday life in Amarna. It was all handled peacefully and depicted in the wall paintings. But let's also look at the relationships created by the local economy, which are also vehicles for opening to the Highest Good. Remember the trade associations and how peace could actually be measured and licensed? This principle was explained over and over again in constantly expanding ways through wall art depicting work. One could interpret the depictions on the walls as saying: "I asked that good be mine. Then this happened to me, and then this, and each was better than the one before." Thus much encouragement and advice for everyone to do the same was readily available. Rather than being an exact translation of the vernacular, the words on the walls were meant to be renditions of the grace of anyone's life.

If the cartoonists of today might begin to tell the old stories all over again in a positive way, it might go like this.

> *"First I was born of a good man and woman in a family of peace, and then I went to a school of Higher Mind and found my own connection to the stars, which directed me to join a trade group of metal workers. This group of well-intentioned workers taught me my trade by being good to me as well as the customers. As my work progressed, I learned more and more about what forging and forming of metal could do to enhance the world around me."*

"Thus I became a craftsman and earned a living. Then my family began with the introduction to a fine girl who came from her family well recommended as having the right intention and we found each other to be true of mind and body. One night we eloped and made our contact with the stars asking for the blessing of the Highest Good upon our union. And thus we were made pregnant on the first occasion to be so. We rejoiced at the number and quality of our children and thus our life being blessed, we did much to enhance the lives of our family and community so that their intentions would be blessed with the best that life had to offer. Each of our children had a different talent and went to school to open their minds completely in peace. There, they made their own contact with the stars and were guided in ways most likely to find their own good, which was good for all of us. "

And thus the intention for the Highest Good unfolds over many thousands of years of our history. And it brings us much joy to be brought back through the loop of life and return again and again. Thus we could not resist the urge to paint on the walls all over again. Some paintings were stories of several lifetimes of a person. The loop of life is depicted as a small stick with an oval wire extending from the handle. As this loop would suggest, once started in one intention for good, all good is brought back to the beginning intention, only to be brought out into another lifetime again and again.

The Loop of Life

And thus it will be for these books, as their intention is so grand as to be accepted by nearly all who are intending the same. And equally delightful, they will be ignored by those intending the reverse of the Highest Good. Thus you will always be in the company of the highest kind of people and no other, bringing you your best happiness of finding that all relationships of the future will be of the Higher Mind and no less.

Indeed all of this has been brought to you out of a decidedly reversal set of experiences meant from the beginning to bring good to all. Even though, in the meantime, there has been discomfort, destruction of much that was valuable to you, and many tears, once you decided that only the best will do, then all that is less must be bypassed. Your lifetimes have much in common, for you have done this over and over again, even if not all are depicted on the walls.

Joyce: I can just see myself walking like an Egyptian on painted walls, telling of my births and deaths, marriages, and children. I would want to get out a paintbrush and tell all about my son, the Revered

Healer. I do hope to go to Egypt one day and see for myself some of the wall paintings. I might want to say: "I remember him. He had such a good lifetime and so many friends. And she was my sister in one lifetime and my mother in another and we loved each other so. These are my family, friends, and countrymen still smiling in white, blue, and brown paint." I might feel as if I were home.

Chapter Seven:
Play It Again, Soul

Joyce: Revered Healer, you talked about seeing your mother's etheric double as a boy and how it changed your thinking. Would you explain more about the etheric double and what it has to do with human life in time and space?

Revered Healer: In the days when we were founding Egypt, I had many experiences that taught me that the universe is good. When I was in Amarna, doing what I did in the person of Akhenaten, I assumed the role of a new kind of king and elected to forget what I had learned before, so thus the stage was open for yet another new beginning to be enacted. Thus I was completely open to seeing earthly existence in a new way. All of it gave me a unique understanding of what the Earth's existence is and what it is not.

   If I could use the analogy of a theater production to explain how a soul comes to earthly existence, I would comment that one could come to the close of a play when the ending is evident and the curtain ready to fall, and say whether it was a comedy or a tragedy and either applaud or boo and throw things. But to make the play happen in the first place, the players had to be completely in the roles that they have elected to play and assume for the purpose of the play that they do not know the ending, although they have all read the script in advance. They have to be the characters, wear the costumes, assume the manners, say the lines, and take the falls. As they play the roles and act out the script, they experience new things and develop new personalities so as to engage the audience in the whole play. Indeed it is considered entertainment even if the story were a tragedy just to be transported into another realm of experience where one can see one's own life in a new way. So it is that souls incarnate in life plans not knowing the outcome in their Conscious Mind, although they do in Higher Mind. As they experience all that takes place, making decisions as they go, they have the opportunity to fall in love with love in a ceaseless encounter with the many faces of God.

More exactly stated, we souls wander through many realms of existence owning the existence of God wherever we go. No matter that it is grim or disgraceful or happy and prosperous. It is our God and we love God wherever He is, so to speak. And since God *is* all existence, there can be nowhere or no time in which he cannot be found and appreciated. Much like a child walking through a hall of mirrors, which changes and distorts his shape, he nevertheless sees himself. One always has the opportunity to see God at all times and circumstances.

Therefore, we come once again to the definition of oneself as a soul who decides to enact a version of itself in a temporary lifetime for the fun of interacting. Again think about a play with actors who are dedicated to the performance of a script. Once one agrees to play the role, one assumes a new name with all of the characteristics involved with the character whether happy or sad in one role, or innocent and pure in the next. Ultimately, it is still the same actor, and the same soul. Thus with the new temporary name of the role, one who is naturally sad might become happy or vice versa. None can truly be harmed, although they appear to be so, for they each have within themselves their true name and identity as an actor to return to at intermission.

Should one show up on stage with the ability to read the mind of the play writer so well that the play writer himself shows up, that is a different kind of play. If the storyteller/play writer is played so clearly and gracefully, that the actor almost doesn't exist, then one has breached all rules of the theater. Such is done when the Conscious Mind allows the soul to speak in all actions. Therefore having such fine cooperation, there is almost no need for players to be players except for the experience and fun of it and so a new form of theater evolved.

In this form of play, not only are the three walls of the theatrical set in place, the back and two sides, but indeed the fourth wall (the wall between the cast and the audience) and even the fifth wall (the wall between the cast and the script writer) will have been broached. For who would show up to be the play writer, but myself, the soul? Who would show up to be the player, but my double – you in your conscious form? And who would be the audience, but the whole lot of us in both conscious forms and super conscious forms? We would all of us be in a great mixture of comedy and tragedy in the act of finding God no matter where the story line goes.

Therefore, if one asks what is the true purpose of life, there is not just one. Each purpose is a variation of expression of where and when one can find God. Once one has this view, one can accept the tragedy of one's life as a variant of another's, which was successful and happy. For both tragedy and success were in existence before the life began. One who leaves physical life can then create a new script, a new lifetime and thus express their particular version of how much they are in love with God. No one is any more blessed than another. However, it does takes a more practiced eye to realize that what is going on is only a theatrical performance involving many participants all of whom are in love with God.

Thus we come to the Amarna Experience, which was the Egyptian Script for a peaceful existence. It was specifically written for the purpose of seeing how long it could last. And indeed, it did last for a very long time in so graceful a way, that those actors who played key roles have signed on for yet another version of the same plot. It is like saying: "Let's get together in the year 2012, like we planned, and start all over again to perform the same play. Only this time we will have to start with a new premise stating that it has all happened before and we are just reliving it in a new way. Then we will all pick new roles and act them out with great joy and happiness and this time, the good guys will win. It will be such a resounding hit that the theater will be closed for renovations for the season, only to be reopened at a later date, in another area of town!"

Therefore, to answer your question, the double that I saw as my Mother was yet another form of herself acting in a new way to impress me with the many ways in which a soul can be active in the physical world. I knew, early on, that my hopes and prayers for peace were entirely possible just because there were so many souls in agreement with the plot. Furthermore, they could enact any form or role that was necessary, including those who could lift heavy stones or even tiny little orb beings who could play the role of particles of rock dust for the time being and then change back to solid rocks later.

Clearly my lifetime as the founder of Egypt was an important one, but it did not stop there. It was followed by another pivotal moment when the much later Amarna Experience became possible. For if I had thought that I could never come back as myself in a new and different form, then the hundred years of peace that I planned for myself during the founding would have been over and then what would I do for fun? In short, as Beings of Light, we can beam ourselves just about anywhere, anytime, and keep the promises that we made. We do this in either etheric form as doubles or in human form as people and sometimes both at the same time.

Joyce: If I had not followed your story from the beginning, I would have found this difficult to believe, but since writing *Book 3: Being of Light*, I can clearly see that we are orbs of light and can go and do whatever we like. We can even at times form a human body, discard it, replace it, and have a great time finding God in all places and circumstances. So just to summarize and hopefully clarify, In terms of the aura, what exactly is the double?

Revered Healer: It is the temporary replication of the aura without the body. Its actions are controlled by the soul, which still resides in the aura. It is a spiritual thing, but is of light, so it can be seen in certain conditions. It is very capable of forming intentions for the body to implement when it has a body, and it can act to some degree on physical objects without a body. It can sense the same things as a body can and the Higher Mind can be aware of these sensations. After its purpose has been served, it contracts back into the aura with a body and continues on until needed or wanted again. Or, if it did not previously have a body, it returns to its original soul's spiritual state. It can only be used for the good as it partakes of the spirit realm.

Joyce: Thanks for that clarification. I know that this is a concept that will take some getting used to, but I'm sure that there are some people who have experienced it and will recognize it immediately. So assuming that the readers have gotten this far and I think that they have, let's ask some pointed questions just to satisfy curiosity. For example, how does one's double recognize itself if it meets itself in etheric or human form?

Revered Healer: Why not ask the double that is sitting behind your chair literally opening the space between your shoulder blades where the truth seal of approval lies for you? For some, this may seem just a place on the back, but for the etheric double, it is a soft spot in the aura that yells and screams, "The truth and only the truth, thank you God." Indeed it attracts many beings of light to come and deposit what information and truth they have to offer for the duty that you perform. Thus you often find that there is a little achy spot in the middle of your back when the truth is not forthcoming or, sometimes, because it is active with much truth. Indeed, many bodily sensations are much like that. Tickles, itches, scratchy skin, rashes, etc. are all openings and closings of spirals in the aura that at times transfer much energy which has to find some way to express itself, so it literally rubs you the wrong way.

Once you open to the true meaning of a sensation, then the sensation usually disappears, leaving much that is certain about a situation or a person's response. Thus there is a certain gut feeling that goes with being alive in human form and it is from this gut or skin feeling that most have their first experience of their own etheric double.

At work in most people's lives is a little peephole of existence that allows them to learn what they need to know to stay alive and to be comfortable. It is usually referred to as survival instinct or intuition given by Higher Mind, which gives instruction to the body directly without conscious thought. For example, one immediately removes one's hand from fire without thought. Without a survival instinct, there would be no human left on the Earth for they would all have been eaten or burned to death in volcanoes or drowned in the sea. This instinct is not the only one that we have, however. There are three. The first instinct is self-preservation and it lasts the entire lifetime of the body. The second instinct is that of pride of workmanship. For if one wants to do or to make something, there needs to be a drive to do it well. The third instinct is the instinct to mate and to reproduce oneself. With this one, we find that the influence of the etheric double that is in back of you is immense.

For who of you has actually understood why on the back of the neck, sometimes the hairs stand up straight and other times, they lay down? This sensation is the presence of an etheric double. In fact, one's etheric double talks directly to one's body about the situation that one is experiencing, leaving the Conscious Mind to figure it out later.

Spirit beings not in incarnation can also use a double. If one had laid one's hand on the throttle, so to speak, of a space ship and flown it to the solar system of the Star Sirius, one would see nothing of physical form that looked human on any of the planets. Yet the Hathors regularly assumed an etheric humanlike form on Earth for the purpose of explaining what they are like. They depicted themselves as female with big braids and cow like ears, but generally a small female human face. Without the spirit forms creating these doubles, we as Egyptians would not have known what to think about them. But because of the care with which they depicted themselves to us, we understood immediately that they meant us no harm and indeed, were very practical advisors of great high wisdom. For example, one of their great gifts was the knowledge of the care and breeding of cattle, which so boosted our diet that we grew quite strong. In addition, the care of the scalp and hair was introduced to us, as our natural hair was thick and unruly. They suggested braiding the hair in spiral patterns that contained the hair, kept it clean and gave us the peaceful energies of the spiral shape around our heads.

Egyptian image of the Hathors

Although the Hathors formed this image for us, we found that, the etheric double can also be literally seen as a ball of light floating in the air or sky, or even as a small magnetic flash of light seen in the eyes. As we pass through the etheric field of light that a human is, we disturb the field and some ions flash the precise color that we are. Thus it is said from time immemorial that what you see is what you get. Once the colors are interpreted, there is much fun to be had to guess who is interacting with your aura. If it is a big flash, there are many of us alike passing through, so to speak.

If we want to ask you a question, then we do through thought-speak (a sudden, benign thought not of one's own construction) and if you answer with heart-speak (a grateful and loving recognition of their beloved presence), then a transaction has occurred. If not, then we just pass on in peace. But once an interaction has occurred, there is an attraction that becomes a moment in time when we can all speak and listen to a human and there is a mutual gain of understanding. If this is done in heart-speak, then the momentum of love is enhanced.

We describe all of this to show that the nature of communication between beings is largely outside the control of the Conscious Mind. By this I mean the Being of Light – the aura – controls the urge to communicate, to love, to change one's lifestyle, and even to mate, not the Conscious Mind. Thus when the songs sing of a bolt of lightening, a flash of light or the Earth moving under one's feet, it is literally a light form or etheric double at work.

Once this is understood, one should never misunderstand that contact with one's soul through bodily sensations is a valid and good thing. Thus living with one's soul, essentially a double, is much like the term falling in love. Once one falls in love, it is hard to see anything in the same way. Also, if falling is not to one's liking, one might also say one rises to meet the energy level of the soul's intention.

Such changes are profound. For example, once a contact for love is made, there is an enduring interest to see the relationship through to its end or risk being unhappy. The loved one immediately appears to be the source of one's happiness and none other. It is literally the opportunity for two balls of light to form a single one and to support and enlighten each other. So satisfying is this type of union, if successfully completed, that one must say good-bye to all others and devote oneself to the Beloved in peace for all of their days and nights, producing children and all of the other needs of their time together. If a union such as this eventually falls apart, its completion is always desired as being very important and its failure regretted.

Thus we find that the double of a person is one's soul at work upon the human frame. If one scratches an itch or works at translating the meaning of a rash or a sneeze, then there is no hope to ever again believe that you and I are not one. For if the soul decides to be in love, then the body falls in love and after loving for a lifetime, if earthy love is not enough, then the death of the body is possible so as to enjoy even more of what one loves to be attained in a new form.

Once one's Beloved is encountered, the work of love is entertained and one's body is at rest in doing the work of the lifetime of love. There is often a very long time of pure enjoyment, just for the taking. We find that indeed, this writer does have a one and only, who is etherically on-line at this time and responding to the calling of his true name. As if by magic, events pass from one to the other and there is never any insult to the gift of giving love and being cherished by the other, and they can remain together for as long as they like.

Nothing will keep them apart, not even death of the body.

And so, it has been from a very long time ago that the names of Akhenaten and his favored one Nefertiti are united as one. And the same being of grace that she was at that time along the living stream of waters found in the Nile is waiting for it to happen again. And when that occurs, they will mark their time by being seated together once again at the farm in warm embrace. With all being forgiven, one cannot even be sure of what it was that had kept them apart or which is yours or mine. As the Revered Healer realized, if we can form ourselves into etheric doubles, then we can do anything.

Chapter Eight:
Will Love, No Harm

Joyce: Revered Healer, you have talked about experiences that we have all encountered, but have little understanding of. You are saying that the soul acts upon the physical body and emotions, creating experiences to which we are moved to respond to in very deep ways. Can you tell me more about how this leads us to live in peace?

Revered Healer: I have led you to an understanding that the physical and spiritual sides of life are intimately interactive. For example, when one comes into existence as a baby, there are parents who care for it on the physical side, but also others who care for it on the etheric side. As a baby feeds at the breast and is carried in the arms, it comes to know that it is loved and cared for. Its survival is not in question, so it settles into rest at night and joyful play during the day. It does not concern itself about the time of day or the cause for anything to happen. It is about as cooperative with spirit and thus happy as a human can get. Babies who are not treated in this manner are indeed caused to be in alarm and never know pure peace in their lifetime. Thus the role of a peaceful mother is a powerful one and should never be overlooked as a cause and foundation for a peaceful society. We ended the prior chapter with the announcement that there is never an ending better than one started in sorrow, but ended in bliss. With this understanding, we bless the union of parents with all of the comings and goings of etheric beings needed to make a union to survive and prosper. Therefore, there is a need to discuss how a great relationship is so blessed.

Joyce: I certainly agree about the role of the mother in a family. It's like the old saying: "If Mother is not happy, then no one is happy." Motherhood is a like a deep well of life which draws up life and pours over during pregnancy and motherhood. If more people appreciated this, there might be more support and care of mothers, especially mothers with small children. When I had my two daughters, I felt so blissfully happy just to be mother and to have those small, beautiful babies that the rest of the world was of little interest. All of the stresses of the rest of life seemed to be easier. I just made the best of the marriage and the energy of life coming from the little family carried us all safely along.

Since I have asked for a good relationship for this part of my life, I am eager to learn more about how such relationships are built upon the Highest Good, maintained, and used to manifest more good.

Revered Healer: So let's know from the start that the role of mother is essentially the transference of life from one dimension to another. In doing this service, the body of a mother is designed to be so full of life and giving of her resources that she literally founds a civilization. This is how Amarna viewed women and their role as mother. A woman was not one to be shown as pretty, thin, and talented and to be given a prize, but rather as to be one appreciated with the same glory as one would an emperor who had conquered new lands. For it is, indeed she and only she, who could populate any land. And in order to do that, she needs to be supported and if she is, then she would thrive herself, giving so much life and energy as to be the origin of a peaceful society.

With this said about the giving of a peaceful start to human life, there is much that can be discussed about how new technology can improve society by supporting the birth process. Let us try to convince the modern world that the world will not turn to the good with machines and electronic devices. It will happen by supporting new life to be good starts in life. We approve the use of such things as contraceptives so that women not prepared to be mothers can delay their reproduction until they can do so in peace. But with a mother ready to conceive, the preparation of the birth canal for such a beautiful process as giving birth needs to be explained.

Once a woman conceives, there are many changes in her body that make her viable for the carrying of a baby. This is a marvelous thing, but it also makes her vulnerable to pressures to perform other duties such as demanding physical work. Thus the role of fatherhood comes to the defense of the mother. By performing the harder duties and providing food, shelter, and protection, he makes her motherhood all the more viable. And by doing so, his seed, which he transported into her birth canal, has the likelihood of being given a strong and peaceful birth. In ancient times, the whole community watched and participated as a new being of light came into physical existence in peace. Thus, like mourners who chant for the leaving of a being of light, the birth singers surrounded the mother in labor to sing the new baby into the community.

With such support and help evident, the parents are assured that if they fail, err, or need assistance, the whole community stands ready to step in and give aid in any form needed. Thus the baby has the support not only of its parents and grandparents, but the whole community that stands ready in any way needed to provide support for this new life. Thus the revered phrase: "It takes a village to raise a child."

With that type of participation, there is never a need that is not provided and thus a small child learns to live in peace and enlightenment from its first breath. With this in place, there is no place that the child can go in the community where he or she is not treated to help, guidance, and open hearts. The idea of the nature of the Highest Good is started early in life and never ends. For Amarna had its problems as any society will have, but the role of the Highest Good provided a way for each and every issue, conflict, or seeming problem to be advanced in a good way. Thus we come to the discussion of the nature of the Highest Good in relationships.

For a relationship to be founded in the proper way, it needs to be intended to be good and never bad from the very beginning. Although this might seem obvious at first glance, as many couples have found, the inclusion of some doubt or self-serving intentions on the part of one or the other can make for a lot of harm later in the relationship. Thus the nature of an intention needs to be explained.

If one intends to make something like a basket, one has to imagine in one's mind what it will be used for, what it will look like, and how it is to be made. Only then does one select the resources available. With this simple analogy in mind, a prospective couple could come to counselors to answer and discuss a set of simple questions. After a lengthy period of thought and discussion, they could submit to their families a written plan for the marriage. With this plan submitted, the members of the local community who have experience with marriage could discuss the limitations involved in the plan. They could discuss and share with the couple the expected outcomes of limited intentions, poor design of living arrangements, or too few resources of character or skills. If such a simple process could be presented in schools where teenage children attend they can begin to think more seriously about the nature of a relationship before they become active in one. With the wise guidance of their parents, and much time and patience, there will be more success. But learning even from failure, those who fail can come back later and find themselves to be more successful and even aid the new comers. Each generation becomes a role model of how it is to be done, displaying many styles and ways for marriages to begin, develop and even end.

With a plan reviewed and supported by the family and community, a marriage can be founded upon better footing. When parenthood is desired, a peaceful birth and childhood is possible. However, once a couple decides to become pregnant, the role of each is again to be discussed, agreed upon, and made clear as far as can be known. The input of other experienced parents will identify areas that might be ignored or under appreciated, such as who takes the child for a walk while the other sleeps, or who changes diapers in the middle of the night. If not discussed before hand, such decisions are made in the heat of a fast changing, stressful period in one's life and there tends to be strife and discouraging words. Indeed the help and assistance of one and all in the family and community is called upon, but not in a way that takes the place of the parents or to relieve them of the unfolding opportunities of such a grace-filled experience. For the unfolding of one's heart and the experiencing of the desire for more love is exactly what it is all about.

And at last, we have the making of a story of grace from which a peaceful society can arise. For it takes children born and raised in peace to build peace into the culture and civilization for long lasting prosperity.

Joyce: I so wish that I had done this before both marriages. It would have revealed areas of disagreement before the marriage was formed and maybe another and better decision could have been made. If so, even the experience of doing the plan would have the benefit of preparing each for finding another partner better suited for such an important experience in one's life. Please continue. I find this so simple and sensible that it would be easy to do.

Revered Healer: For one to be addressed in any relationship as a Beloved One, there must be one who has the integrity to have gone to their Higher Mind for one more step. In this step, there is an agreement with the Higher Mind of each party to discuss the nature and purpose of the entire lifetime of each party. Indeed, relationships that are the culmination of the work of several lifetimes, all guided by a single intention, is a magnificent achievement for any soul to achieve. Thus the makers of the intention to be in relationship with each other must have some idea of their own intentions for the present lifetime as well as the several before. To do this effectively, those trained in the skill to access multiple layers of consciousness where the Akasic records lie ready to be opened, come forward to do past life readings. With such a consultation, one is assured that one's intentions in this lifetime are of the Highest Good for both parties and that one supports and completes the other.

Peaceful One: Which type of lifetime would you like me to read for you, my dearest one, for I know that you hunger to know?

Joyce: You always know what I want and need and anticipate it so well. Yes, I would like to know the intention for my current lifetime and the relevant lifetimes that support and continue that single intention.

Peaceful One: Well, then, we must turn the pages of this great book about the lifetimes of your soul. Some of the pages have your current name and others have old names, so we must peruse all and determine which are the lifetimes that you will need to make peace with this life and the coming relationship.

After a long time thumbing page after page, we come upon the current one as Joyce McCartney and wonder why you have ceased to know that the beginning of your name starts with the word joy. For you were not intending in this lifetime to be poor or rich, married or unmarried, only joyful in the pursuit of the Highest Good. Thus we find that the written record says you have come to a good understanding of the early life experiences of denial of joy. These experiences of loss started when you were a little girl in need of your parents' attention, but were denied it in so many ways, because of the demands of a very large family and your mother's illness. Later, a very strict religious teaching enhanced the belief that denial and restrictions of love were good for a child to get used to.

Thus we find, that at this point in this lifetime, there is an event of the nature that is the reverse of the earlier events. It is planned to have those who have been waiting to be participants of this life returning to do just that. Thus, we find the attention of the father and mother lost in early life replaced in the burgeoning family of the daughter and her husband. In addition, your good friend who recently passed away was sent to bring joy and laughter of companionship to your work life. Finally, we find that the long guarded identity of your mate will be revealed soon. With this addition to your experience, you will have little to experience but the joyful noise of your family returned. Exemplified as a Doer of the Highest Good is a good way to state this lifetime.

In a prior lifetime, we find that your joy was made whole and complete by being a doctor's wife around the time of the American Civil War. At the end of the war, you and your husband ended up in a rural area, making your home a peaceful and happy one. You spent most of your time tending and harvesting your fruit trees, the many herbs of which your husband was enamored and the tending of the many babies you enjoyed. Remarkably, the couple lived in the same state as you live at this time.

In this lifetime, you and he made do with much less happiness in the beginning of the lifetime, so as to serve the needs of the many wounded and made sorrowful by the war, but made the intention to be together in peace after that. Thus it will be the same for this lifetime, for the two are the same participants and have the same intentions for this lifetime together, just different issues. Instead of a war, this lifetime has the issues of false relationships and the need for social reform to be addressed. There are plans to start farming methods and a lifestyle similar to that described in the record of Amarna.

Now we proceed into yet another lifetime before ancient Egypt turned the corner to the time of the Pharaohs, namely, the lifetime of RaTa and his compatriots. In this lifetime, you were RaTa's assistant and your mate was his Health Counselor. The Musician Healer ably assisted you both. Together, they helped to rejuvenate RaTa from an old man to a young and vital man in his twenties. Together they assisted RaTa to develop the Highest Good in Egyptian society and to rejuvenate himself. Thus you and your mate devoted your younger years to that effort, but later you became a retired couple living in peace for the last half of your lives in joy and friendliness. You wanted to be an example to all comers who wanted to know how the experiences of those living the lifestyle of the Mystery Schools was being manifested. While much can be learned about how the Mystery Schools were conducted, suffice it to say that the teachings of the Mystery Schools needed to be not only learned, but also lived.

Thus in coming back to the current lifetime, there are many who will be returning to the Amarna Experience of the day only to find the loving couple still at work in deep concentration as to how the Highest Good will be made whole in each and every action of the day. Your farm will raise amazing peaches, apples, and pears in unlikely weather. The herb garden will produce leaves, seeds, and stems with the power to heal much that is amiss in society today. As in the prior lifetimes, when the two met, amazing things start to happen and it is so in this one. Once the signal has been sent such as the publishing of the story of Amarna, more wonderful things will transpire and indeed the story of Amarna will be replicated all over again.

And so it is with this small, but impressive view of your lifetime intention being played out over millennia of time that we come to the final story of good coming from The Amarna Experience. We will describe how yet another culture was raised from the dusty fields of Africa, building first a small farm, followed by a village and ending in a worldwide culture to be emulated many years later.

Joyce: Although I have often been surprised in these readings, this one outdoes them all. In a couple of pages, you have told my lifetimes, introduced me to my mate, told the future of our society to be in peace and opened the opportunity for many others to get their past life readings so as to join in relationships of so much potential for happiness and peace that they are a blessing.

Wow, wow and wow. I have to think about this one.

You are saying that there is another Amarna Experience that I participated in. And now I am recreating how the Highest Good can be used as a foundation for a social order at my farm. I can't imagine what you have next for me, but I know that it will be good.

Revered Healer: So much has been made available to us to reveal through your careful and constant attention in doing these readings, that we are graced, as well as you. Do not call yourself a hermit, rather a retriever of the great record of peace. So do go on. We love being here with you as much as you do.

Joyce: Apparently we have been together a very long time and probably forever yet to come. I have to think about this, but thanks for being there with me. I love you.

Chapter Nine:
Do It Again in Dogon

Joyce: Since we have been in physical existence over and over again and are still doing it, I can only guess that we had a high purpose. We certainly had fun. I am starting to get used to this idea. So what else happened?

Revered Healer: Do not think that the lifetime of Akhenaten and his wife Nefertiti were the only times that a peaceful society was attempted on the Earth, for all cultures admired the Egyptian one and did their best to access their Higher Minds to release their grief and acquire benign information. But few succeeded as well as the descendants of the long line of Mystery School teachers who later left Egypt to travel the world in search of places that had a great need for their services.

Once dealers in trade goods came requesting help to found another society in a desolate place, the presence of Great Mother was demanded. Thus Great Mother left Egypt and wandered with roving bands of natives of the inner continent of Africa in search of a place so destitute of any other life that no one would ever believe that life could exist there.

The Great Mother and a small band of her followers left Amarna with great fanfare, bidding good-bye to their families and friends who removed her image from their carved walls and traveled under the watchful eye of the Hathors. They were guided to cross the great continent of Africa and to settle in a dry and arid place now called Dogon in Mali. This place was far away from any source of water and not a patch of shade or shoot of grass was to be found. It was essentially a dusty patch of ground about fifty miles across.

After their arrival, the small band of about fifteen people settled in tents for the night. A bright band of stars appeared on the horizon and zigzagged across the sky. All but one of them seemed to fade, leaving the one named the Dog Star seeming to dazzle the eye of the Great Mother. Accessing her Higher Mind, Great Mother requested to hear from the beings that inhabited the star system. With that, the Hathors introduced their cousins; the bear-shaped ones later named the Dogon Gods. With these great beings in friendly communication, the residents were guided to the trash heap of the last residents who had lived there before them, leaving their trash around in the form of broken pottery.

When found, these little shards of pots were interpreted as being directions for the discovery of much that was available in the area. For example, the shards showed pictures of the little animals that inhabited the tunnels beneath the sand called geckos that could be followed to find the best places for water. These friendly little lizards living beneath the ground gave Great Mother directions as to where to find good water and indeed a good well was dug.

As soon as the water flowed, there was a need to make more pots for using the water, so the discarded potshards were examined to see what kind of soil had been used in their making and how far away it was to be found. Soon they found a drawing of a little man making his way to the local mud hole, digging the mud, and forming pots. Thus the new locals started digging wherever they found a slightly muddy depression, until they found clay suitable for forming pottery.

With this, they needed a way to fire the formed pots. And so, the request for a way to fire the pots was presented to the bear gods. These spirit beings gave directions to dig a round pit and to line it with the old shiny shards so as to reflect the sun, much like a bowl shaped solar reflector today. The pots were placed in the heat and the hot sun soon fired the pots. At the end of the process, water was splashed on the hot pots forming steam, which caused the pots to be glazed. Thus the people had pots to both carry water and to cook food.

As people took instruction from Great Mother and established their own channel to the etheric plane, they began to address their other needs. For example, they needed to build houses appropriate for the intense heat of the day and cold at night. They were given directions by the Bear Gods as to the type of dirt that could be formed into glazed slabs to be used for building houses.

They formed bricks and slabs in molds and fired them the same as the pots. Then they contacted the gods for the best design for their homes and were instructed to build them so that the morning sun evaporated the dew on the roof and sides causing cooling by evaporation. They noticed the effect and enhanced it by wetting down the slabs on the south side of the house for the afternoon sun to evaporate, again causing cooling.

Within a few weeks of this cooling system being effective, they learned that the catching of the mist and dew on the rooftops and letting it run down the south side was the easiest way to get the cooling effect, so they installed a form of roofing made from straw tubing and gutters. The net effect was a constant dripping in the morning to saturate the outside walls, but not flood them. The hotter the sun, the cooler the insides of the houses were and since the glazed slabs were good insulators, the effect would last until evening when the desert turned suddenly very cold. But the cold did not penetrate the small house since a form of a shutter and door prevented loss of the interior mild air. The slabs were so successful being hard and shiny, they were found to be easy to clean, easy to stack and made for such good insulation that everyone was impressed with the good advice from the Bear Gods.

As the small community used the slabs to build the walls, they found that the problem of finding materials for strong roof rafters needed the help of the Bear Gods. Consultation with the star beings alluded to the fact that the timbers needed were not local and thus formation of a trading economy was necessary. In order to trade, it was needed to have something of value to trade for the timber from those who had it to give. Thus an improved method of forming pottery was given by the star beings in which pots, buckets, plates, cups, and even utensils was vastly improved, all of then heated in the sun kiln. In addition to new forming methods including twisting and turning the mud in circles so as to fine tune the shape and construct a stronger container, the decoration of the items was so unique and beautiful that the new products became known and valued for miles around. Thus a trading circle was formed in which people who had timber and wanted the dinnerware arrived in numbers enough to make the construction of strong roofs possible.

Soon, there were many such houses, some still available for excavation today, which housed the people in perfect comfort and safety. We mention safety, for it was the habit of the moon and star watchers to stay up late, seated on the rooftops and record the passing of the cycles of the moon. During these hours, the hyenas and jackals would often came to call, looking for a late meal, so rooftop observation posts were constructed for safe star gazing. The measuring of the moon's rotation was recorded on long strips of cloth made from strings of vegetable fiber. These recordkeeping scrolls were made from the instructions of the bear gods. These scrolls contained calibrations to show the wobble of the moon in minute detail. Thus the difference in the distance between the moon and the Earth could be predicted in a precise manner. Soon the community learned, as had the Amarna community, that the times when the moon was closest to the Earth were good times for conceiving new children and planting seeds.

In addition, the southern most passing of the sun was documented. It was known that the sun is the most important influence over plant life and openings to channel. The lowest point of the southern sun indicated the decline of one form of energy from the sun. Then, as the sun sets low for one day and starts rising the next, it brings in another type of energy. The newly rising southern sun activates seeds, creates better emotional states, and engenders the ability to channel. Seeds were ready to plant at the equinox as well as a favorable emotional state for channeling. This ancient knowledge of the influence of the position of the sun was given by the star beings and had been practiced in Amarna. But it was also well known in other parts of the ancient world and passed down from generation to generation. In many of the great monuments all around the world are found standing stones, which show these two positions of the sun. More information about this sun position technology will be given when requested by those interested enough to inquire.

And so the houses used as observatories at night were one- to two-story ceramic-coated structures with wood floors and a wood frame roof covered mostly with rubble to reflect heat during the day and hold it during the night. Essentially a rock structure, they were very much like the underground Egyptian tunnels of old and were left intact for very long periods of time, some even able to be excavated today. From these ancient homes built on good advice, much can be learned even today about how housing in modern times can be energy efficient and less costly to build.

Combining modern solar powered electricity collection technology together with the methods of living with these simple ancient methods, offers many possibilities for creating a local and benign way to live in peace with all life forms. Even in cold climates, the sun's rays can be collected in the summer to form and fire ceramic-coated building materials of local soil. Glass blocks can be used for light. Such bricks, slabs, and blocks can be placed in any size building or structure up to two floors to suit the needs of the occupants and the local climate. Such houses can be arranged in small communities with gardens worked with shared resources and labor. Others might be built in remote areas for solitary lifestyles or even resorts for rest and recreation. Such communities would provide people housing without the need for stressful jobs to support expensive housing and expansive lifestyles. With guidelines similar to these, for the Highest Good, peaceful living would produce many more inventions as well as peaceful participants for future generations.

For example, with the addition of a solar water heater on the roof of such a home, which recycles water for bathing and heating, much cost can be saved. Along with water, recycling air channels drawing air from the ground for summer cooling and winter heating on the roof can contribute to a simple, but profoundly satisfying lifestyle that can continue to bless the earth. In very cold climates a tank of methane gas from recycled trash can be used as supplement heat. Upon application by interested persons wishing to discuss these peaceful ways of being, much information of this nature will be given and shared worldwide. To do so would cause a revolution in housing from high cost, energy users to low cost, energy conservers. With solar electric cells, homes can become electric producers. Thus every family can afford a home and even make a living by selling its unused electricity all over the world through the existing electric grid.

Without pressures to make and spend money, people will have the time, rest, and inspiration to do creative, healing, and instructional activities and to build better relationships worldwide. Since all of this low tech advice has been given previously and used in prior societies, except for the existence of electric motors of which there were none in ancient days, there is more than enough evidence to show that it can indeed be done again in new and creative ways in modern times.

To return to the story of ancient Dogon, there was enough leisure for the past life readers to make a living. For when the soul has the option to begin again in a new body, it needs a union between a man and a woman in a good relationship, thus the need for many to be married and prospered through the art of child bearing and child rearing. Thus it can be said that indeed it takes a village of peacekeepers to raise a peaceful child. The ancient village elders were not so much the keepers of the old wisdom, but rather the remainders of the last generation to tell the stories of those who have passed over. And in the telling and retelling, there are some who recognized their own prior lives and are graced to see the comparative nature of one life to succeed another. With this accomplished, the transmission of tribal history is recorded in long telling stories much of which is still in existence. But for the telling abilities to remain in tact, there must be some who have the memory to recall such long stories.

Thus we find that the Akasic Record keepers on the etheric side were drafted from the long line of talented storytellers of Earth experience and vice versa. And so with so much valuable experience, earthly storytellers returned to etheric existence attending to the memories of the new earthly storytellers. Therefore, we invite those of the historical and genealogical interest today to ask for their etheric assistance as well and to be invited into the etheric libraries as well as the physical ones. Indeed the Internet of inner space is much more spacious and easy to use than those of physical existence for there is to be found the great library of experiences and lovers of life about which we speak.

Thus we find that the long journey of the Great Mother into the center of Africa to found yet another society on the best of intentions with the greatest of advice, created a strong a vibrant community of peacekeepers. And thus it will be done again.

While there is much more to tell and many who will come asking, there is yet a much higher place to visit so as to perceive how much good can yet be given with so simple a device as some paper and ink. And so we return our tired author to her peaceful yard full of singing birds and blooming flowers to ponder her travels of inner space. As she listens to our guidance, she will find much that is of joy and still unknown to modern mankind until the returnees recognize themselves and come asking. As she has been given the gift of opening others to their own strong channel to the world of friendly beings, the many who sit in sunny windows reading and asking for help will find that the wonders of her tale are made available to them as well.

+

Joyce: Dear Reader, I think that you would agree that we have traveled a long time through history in this book and have found that at every turn, we were amazed at the strength of the intention for the Highest Good to build great societies from nothing and to endure great setbacks and still survive, not only intact, but even stronger than before. So now you can see why we have met on these pages, which were initially started in such grief and loss that I could not see any good at all. Was I like Cleopatra who accepted the defeat of one form of society for the resurrection of a better one? Did I decide on one level to give up all that I had to make the deepest and most pure relationship that any human can have? If so, I did it unknowingly. I thought that I was in deep trouble and was just asking for the Highest Good for my life because I had no other option. Even in such circumstances, I was immediately given the great gift of opening to Higher Mind. And with that gift, all of the rest of this great story followed. What a surprise!

And then, as I got to know The Peaceful One and felt the nature of the one that I had met, I shivered with respect, love and appreciation. Never knowing what would come next, I moved forward, step by step, to see a bit more, to feel more deeply and to be more blessed. I think that I have only just begun. With the hint that there is a higher place to go to seek even higher information, I can only look forward with blind, but delighted anticipation.

Then we met on these pages and we discovered together the great power that peace is. It can take one little seed, as the story of the mustard seed in the Bible says, and build a whole society from it. Was your little seed the interest in something called good, even The Highest Good? Was it the peaceful and calm advice coming from The Peaceful One? Was it the hope that you would find answers to your own problems? Or did you just want a good friend? A page pal? That and much more was given to you. And now you have the prospect to **be** much more as a result of your readership.

Now that we know what peace can do with so little work or effort, what is our desire? Is it to be more healthy, more compassionate, or just to enjoy what we have? Would you include in your intentions, the existence of all beings on earth to live in peace? For that would be good, indeed a Highest Good. From that high a point of good, in the stratosphere, we could look down with kindness and security and wean ourselves from our fears and grief. Indeed grief would become an antique idea, no longer in use. Now is the time for you to choose. Choose for yourself and all for whom you have come to care.

And so, Dear Reader, we must part for a short while. Although we paged forward together without any idea of the ending, would you agree with me that the journey has been a good one, the ending destined to be good, and, of course, the companionship superb? What has it cost us, indeed, but our woes, regrets, grief and illness? Has it not healed us, saved us more loss and filled our pockets and hearts with grace? We have no reasonable choice but to move on in peace.

As this is the sixth volume of this series of books on the Highest Good, I have no idea of what will come next, but you can be guaranteed that it will be even better and indeed a wonderful, amazing surprise. I will miss you for a while but, until we meet here again in black and white on these pages, I bid you good-bye for now.

Acknowledgements

As the author of this most unusual book, I would like to acknowledge the pioneering contributions of other channeled works. Each author with the courage to both contact their Higher Minds and to publish it to the public has made a very personal contribution to us all.

Therefore, I mention first and most foremost, Edgar Cayce and his legacy organization, the Association for Research and Enlightenment (the ARE) in Virginia Beach, Virginia. In thousands of documented individual readings, this humble man unleashed the vast resources and love of the Great Oneness in modern times. Most of the readings were for healing, others were about history, metaphysics, and reincarnation. Without his work, we would have been strangers to what was so easily available to all. Contact: edgarcayce.org. If you go to The ARE in Virginia Beach, you will find a friendly and knowledgeable staff, library, bookstore, meditation garden, spa, and conference schedule.

Since then, other authors have stepped forward with their own access to Higher Mind. These include:

Neal Donald Walsh: *Conversations With God*

Paul Solomon: *The Readings of the Paul Solomon Source*

Jane Roberts: *The Seth Material*

Gordon Smith: *Developing Mediumship*

Sonia Choquette: *Soul Lessons and Soul Purpose*

Esther and Jerry Hicks: *The Abraham Material*

Tom Kenyon: *The Hathor Material*

Eckert Tolle: *A New Earth*

Oprah Winfrey: She is, herself, the book of the Highest Good in conversation with the public heart.

In regard to contact with nature, I make note of the work of **David Spangler and the Findhorn Project**.

I am grateful for the work of these and many other authors and researchers and greet all who are yet to come.

In addition, there are archeologists, scientists, engineers and architects who have devoted their efforts to uncovering the physical evidence for the ancient culture of Egypt and I wish to acknowledge their work as well. The following are of particular interest to me:

Carmen Boulter, who asks all of the right questions and gathers together those who wish to find the truth.

Laird Scranton, who researched the Dogon heritage.

Mark Lehner, who measures and records the sites so carefully.

Peter Tompkins, who looked so carefully at the Great Pyramid with faith in his heart.

Robert Bauval, who made the connection with the stars and the monuments.

John Anthony West, who sought the high wisdom of ancient Egypt.

Christopher Dunn, who foresaw many of the future uses of the Great Pyramid.

There are many others whose work I have not had time to explore, but I am confident that they will all receive some benefit from the information in these books.

Helping me to write, edit, and produce my books are: **Amy Lee, Peggy Cross, Adam Brown,** and **Phil Crabtree.** I offer my many thanks for your insightful questions, professional skills, and friendship.

Joyce McCartney

www.ingramcontent.com/pod-product-compliance
Lightning Source LLC
Chambersburg PA
CBHW071052090426
42737CB00013B/2334